On to happiness
How life finds us

I wish to thank the clients and students of the Energy School, but first and foremost I wish to thank life, which has allowed me to experience all of this.

Martin Brune

On to happiness

How life finds us

Bibliografische Information der Deutschen Bibliothek:
Die Deutsche Bibliothek verzeichnet diese Publikation in der Deutschen
Nationalbibliografie; detaillierte Daten sind im Internet über
<http://dnb.ddb.de> abrufbar.

© 2007 Martin Brune
Herstellung und Verlag: Books on Demand GmbH, Norderstedt
ISBN: 978-3-8334-6091-3

Inhalt

Preface

There is none. We start immediately. We have no time to lose. The reason will become clear at the end.

A book…?

Elenor

I cannot see the lake, but I can discern it from the soft babbling of the tiny waves. There is fog everywhere, and the condor sits on a bare tree that stands right next to the shore. I can smell it, the lake. The water smells musty – like wood. Wood, I think. I can hear wood moving, creaking. Like the floorboards of an old sailing boat. The condor is perched there on the tree that looks black. Its eyes reflect shock and helplessness at the same time. Everywhere is enveloped in fog. That's why the condor cannot fly. Because it can't see.

I take the fog out of the scene; the fog slowly disappears and the picture becomes clearer. Down there at the lake shore lies a boat – that's where the musty smell and the creaking are coming from. There is a woman lying inside the boat. She is pregnant. She is wearing a dress that seems to be from another century. On the far side of the lake I can see a house burning. The air smells of smoke. The woman is dying.

„Where do you come from?", I ask.

„From the house over there", she says in a weak voice.

„What happened?"

„We were attacked. We are very wealthy, and my husband's brother, who is a good-for-nothing, has always envied us…"

„Where is your husband?"

„He is dead. Everyone is dead. My husband's brother only wanted money, but the argument turned violent. The curtains caught fire and …"

„And?… and?", I ask. She can hardly speak now – she is too exhausted.

„Good-for-nothing!", I think and look at her dress. It is covered in blood. 18th century, I would say. „Good-for-nothing" – somehow it fits, I conclude, and move on.

The condor watches the happenings and wants to be free. It wants to be free from this terrible scene.

„What's your name?", I ask the pregnant woman in the boat again.

„Caroline de Metier", she whispers in a weak voice.

„Caroline, do you want to see the light? You have been here at the shore of the lake for so long – over two hundred years. Do you want to see the light? Do you want to be free at last?", I ask.

Silence. Calm. Strong wing beats resound above the lake, returning with an echo. The condor becomes unsettled, beating its wings, as though it has to fly away and can no longer wait.

„Yes…", she says quietly. „I've been waiting for salvation for such a long time. I don't want to be here any more. Please, take me and my unborn baby to the light."

Suddenly I see two spirits in the picture. They take hold of the woman, lift her from the boat holding her gently under the arms, and disappear with her along a channel of light which stretches from the boat up towards the sky.

Seconds later the lake, the tree, and the burning house disappear. The condor takes off, flies away. It is free again. What remains is pure light. Pure energy. It is as though I was looking at a spinning wheel of light. Warm light. Pleasant.

The treatment is over. „Oh Martin – this is just unbelievable", says Elenor and begins to cry after I tell her what I have seen in her: the dying Caroline de Metier, probably one of her ancestors, and the terrible events by the lake, which had obviously been passed on from generation to generation, and which have been resolved now.

By the way, the condor is one of the most significant creatures in shamanic mythology. It symbolizes vision. It can fly ahead to the place one reaches when one is free. It can overlook the entire scenery. Then it returns to report where the journey will take us. The condor is the harbinger of the life contract which we all have within us, the scout for the place which is ours in this world: the lived life's dream.

But all of this is no longer important to Elenor herself. Because now the condor is flying again.

The suitcases still stand in the hall of my institute. Having just returned from a series of lectures I gave in Vienna, I arrived punctually for our consultation at eight o'clock in the evening. Treatment over the telephone. Elenor is a client from Los Angeles, one the most successful women shamans in North America. They need treatment too, for they come into contact with a lot of people, which often leaves them exposed to extreme energies.

Despair and a sense of grief were "her issues", she told me during the first brief telephone conversation: the permanent

11

feeling of grief and of "somehow being inhibited": stagnation in life.

During the subsequent session Elenor resolves her life stagnation herself: she and her husband have been trying to conceive a child for over 15 years. It hasn't worked. She has had three miscarriages, so she has pushed aside the idea of having a baby. Still, she would never have thought possible that her despondency, her frustration and the sporadic feeling of senselessness in life could be caused by the energy disturbance of a pregnant woman, which manifests itself as the lake and the other visions, although she herself works as a shaman.

All these years she has been feeling like this condor. And the powerlessness of the pregnant woman in her abdomen has also been a constant companion.

By now, you must be surprised. What is all this he is writing here? This nonsense is supposed to have healed Elenor? For heaven's sake! The suspension of this disbelief will take place through this book. However, my aim is certainly not to impress the reader with the things I see and undertake during treatment, because, basically, that is irrelevant. The clients do not have to concern themselves with the images at all. I wouldn't even need to describe these images to them, but naturally every client is curious about who or what is or has been haunting their energy field. Even when Elenor subsequently draws a parallel to her desire to have a baby, this analogy is not influential to the healing, but only in the manner that the woman in the image finds peace and that the condor can fly again. It is another level. A level of images. Energy that informs through images. Now her chakra is cleared from the dark stains.

More nonsense, you may think. By the way, in the meantime Elenor has become pregnant.

Since I started to work as a shaman and founded the school and the institute, I have had no time at all. I enjoy my occupation infinitely. The consultations are extremely successful. And: I must write a book about it. About energy medicine – about how energy medicine works.

At the same time I must continue to write my story – the sequel of the first part, "The Doubter and the Healer", could quite easily be titled "From a Healer to a Shaman without Much Effort on my Part". But I still have both feet on the ground: Hello, I am Martin Brune. I still wear the same clothes as before, I don't wear flowing white guru togas or the gentle permanent smile of a good man on my face, have no Spirit Centre and make no promises.

I think that writing books really is reserved for humans with a lot of staying power and an extreme urge for research. So what am I doing writing one? Is it just because I have many students and clients (the word "patient" is reserved for physicians) who often ask me when will I write a book and published?

What are the book's intentions? To make money is not one of the aims. To spread the knowledge? Yes, perhaps, it could be that. If it serves that purpose I will be happy to write it. Even though "knowledge" cannot be prescribed just like that. And because nature has not actually provided for illness, the book must be kept short – why should a great big book or even many books about illnesses and their treatment be necessary? Trust me, nature intended an easier way.

The preparation

When I wrote my first text "The Doubter and the Healer" and placed it on the Net for downloading, I had no idea how much interest it would evoke among the readership. I am still overwhelmed. On average, some 4,000 users from around the world download the PDF file from the website every month. And I am equally overwhelmed, and I say this with humility and respect, by the success of my treatments.

These are the two reasons for continuing to tell my story. The first is the incredible feedback from my clients, both in quality and in quantity. The second is my path – an overwhelming experience – from one who has been healed to a healer who, step by step, finds his feet in the world of shamans without consciously choosing it – and in doing so experiences things that I would not have thought possible. There is one thing I wish to say beforehand: as soon as something changes in our energy field, everything around us changes – above all the quality of life. This is what happened in my life. At the end of energetic healing processes you will find "happiness", which is your life contract that has at last been liberated thanks to the energy healing. Exactly as it happened to me.

You can read my chronological development in the "El Mundo Espiritual" (The Spiritual World) chapters, and what happened and why in the individual chapters of the three parts: HAPPINESS AND DESTINY; ENERGY, IMBALANCE, HEALING AND CONNECTING; TREATMENT, DESTINY AND HAPPINESS).

No one has to "believe"

I do not want to and will not tell you what you have to believe. You will not be drawn into an unfathomable course that has no end. A healing session with my clients takes no longer than thirty minutes and is carried out a maximum of three times in the beginning. We don't even have to draw the curtains in the room. The phrase "whether you believe it or not" is irrelevant in shamanism. After the session you can forget everything about it. You don't need to interpret things, pursue the issue, you don't need to ponder, reason or think about it. I have already removed it.

It's natural to try to see rhyme or reason in it. In what? Perhaps in the fact that we suddenly feel better after the treatment; that the neurodermatitis disappears; that the constant quarrelling with your mother is automatically settled; that you suddenly receive an offer for a job which you have always wanted and have never been able to get.

Essential is the fact alone that this type of healing has been successful thousands of times. Confirmation that testifies to this can be found in the second part of the book, in the testimonials of clients who believe it is right. And this is exactly the intention of the book: the treatment works. It's as simple as that. It is a tool that can spare us decade-long processes of "work on oneself", bad conscience, misery or accusations (towards one's parents, for example). What is more, one doesn't even have to believe in it. Welcome, dear sceptics.

Live one's own dream

And when "things get going", energy medicine can make one happy. Many of my clients have said that the parameters of their life changed, as though a compass had readjusted the cardinal points.

Most of us do not live our life's dream. We have a job, but actually we've always wanted to be a musician, a writer, a gardener, or just work with other people. We have a partner, the relationship with whom works reasonably well but only to some extent, and what is missing from it we find elsewhere. We have the city we live in, from which we have wanted to get out of for a long time, but the dream of life in the countryside is still hanging above us like a question mark.

Only few – Mozart, Goethe, Prince, Bill Gates, to name but a few, highly talented people of their respective times – start at an early age to live and work in full possession of their pure energetic powers. To them, what they do is not "hard" work. Because they work with their gift – and have done so from an early stage in life.

On average, most of us experience our real destiny at the age of forty years, because that is when a drastic experience often occurs, such as an illness, the loss of a partner, or simply a midlife crisis. But because nothing has happened for a long time, we keep moving according to the same patterns. And we are surprised because nothing changes, because we continue to move in a circle rather than forward, or, for example, because each new partner brings along the same problems.

This is why I am writing this text. It does not heal. Nor does it offer advice. It reports what has happened to me since I became a healer and what happened along the way. This however gives the book the character of a presentation of evidence. Evidence of powers at work, which, when observed from the outside, have a tremendous effect. But I can observe them from the inside. I have learned to see energies and work with them. But let's take things one by one.

This is the story of my biography as a shaman, of the effect a successful energetic therapy has on the client's meaning of life, on "finding" one's destiny in the form of a vocation, love, or any other areas of life.

What is being described here makes this booklet different from other texts whose aim is to teach healing methods, from Ayurveda to Reiki. Healing is only done in practice, not in the head. And anyway, healing is not what this is primarily about. What is more important is that through our healing we find the happiness we have always been searching for.

Those who heal are right, says a proverb

I owe it to the pressure my students put me under that this stock-taking has come into being as a booklet. With this text I give them something back. So far, I have treated some 5,000 clients. And it is only through the feedback of these clients that I know that what I tell them is true and right.

Everything that is written here has happened. Therefore there is nothing in this book that one could not understand or grasp. These are results. You must believe me, I needed a lot of time myself to understand it all. And yet this is knowledge which also existed in Europe a long time ago, including Germany. It is knowledge we have lost through various culture-historical events. But this "primal knowledge" slumbers deep inside us and needs only to be brought back to the surface.

In the Energy School I teach how to reclaim the enormous powers of intention and intuition – in the "Seeing" course one learns how to see energies. In this way one's own wounds, indisposition, pain, or illnesses are transformed into sources of power. One learns to resolve unfavourable life circumstances and find a happy, healthy and prosperous future.

"Healing" is a word I would like to banish from our vocabulary. Illness takes up far too much space in our world. Also, healing implies that we are ill. But are we really ill? Nature did not provide for "illness", as we call it, at all. In shamanic tradition the topic of "illness" occupies only a fraction of the time we have to live, and even less of that to think. The aim is to live our dream, for ourselves and for our children!

It is not our task to regard life as a "path of illness", as our western civilization has ingrained into us almost as a matter of course. Life is about healthy growth, which is also the way of nature. The main responsibility of our existence is therefore to cultivate the field of our life – with the power of vision.

A better expression for "illness" or "healing" is: we are not yet on the correct path. Painful rocks still lie about, and they have to be removed. Only when we heal our wounds can we find a future that brings happiness and achieve growth.

The solution is easier than we think. So easy that the things I write here must strike a decent reasonably educated person as odd. And that's exactly what it is to some extent... the "philosopher's stone" more or less lies in front of our door – provided we are prepared to turn our world view upside down.

HAPPINESS AND DESTINY

El mundo espiritual uno

After I had returned to Germany I often thought of Don Humberto. He was the one who had relieved me from my terrible illness. "Eres mi hermano", he'd said to me: "You are my brother". What did that mean? Was I connected with him now? Was it an honour – or was it just talk?! Does he say that to everyone?

Cologne seemed very strange to me after my healing experience. The city was loud, wet and dark. Energetically dark. And my apartment was the same. The pictures on the wall, the chairs, the tables, the cabinets, the ornaments on the window sills: all junk. It was all stuff from the past, I thought when I returned to my apartment.

Over the following days I cleared up. I threw out more or less half of the furnishings. Until it was bright. "The interior manifests itself on the exterior", I remembered that Humberto told me once, "never the other way round."

I missed the Q'ero.

How can we find happiness?

It is not easy to put energy medicine into words. Moreover, energy medicine, or, rather, spiritual medicine, as I prefer to call it, is about a lot more than just healing, illness, or improvement.

It is about everyone's future. About one's destiny, in the sense of achieving self-realization. Our healing is a basic precondition for this.

When we become really healthy, we can attain, can live our destiny. Because then we are released from all unnecessary burdens, be it fears, doubts, indisposition, or physical complaints. Because then all our life parameters change, in the same way that we abandon old habits when we marry, or think and live differently when we have a baby – this is exactly how things change around us when our energy can flow freely.

Conversely, our life is composed of all "internal" parameters that surround us. A simple example: if you dislike driving your car for long distances, you will be largely bound to your home. Finding a better job would be impossible if it required a long journey by car. So, because of your anxiety, you stay with the same job. We come to terms with our problems and develop avoidance strategies in order not to confront our fears.

If on the other hand we are really healthy, and only few of us are, then we can only attract healthy thoughts, because then deficient thinking does not exist.

Ninety-nine percent of my clients suffer from this sense of inadequacy or fear. The fear that one day they will no longer have enough money, not enough to eat or enough air to breathe – that there will be not enough of something or other in their lives. Many fear that love may go or, even worse, never come back. If we are healthy, then these fears do not exist. During the first stage of the "Seeing" course at the Energy School we work on this fatalistic way of thinking and eliminate it "energetically". Energy fills the spaces these dark stains occupied – your life's energy, so to speak. And through this the actual life contract comes to light.

Should I write about it? Is it interesting? Should the readers know these things? Is the word "destiny" not too religious? Is it not too strongly connected with "fate" and thus with some kind of sacrifice? Should I write that many people who booked my courses have found their destiny? Perhaps I should write about the Energy School being much more than a healing school – actually a life school, in which people can learn to fulfil their life with energies?

I cannot answer all these questions now – I can't make up my mind. So I will drive to the institute first. Today I have 16 sessions – a normal working day.

Franziska

I begin with Franziska. Her issue is an enormous resentment for her parents-in-law who refuse to accept her, and even less her work. In their eyes, she is just one of those "Yoga freaks". Their attitude is condescending and they talk about her with her husband behind her back. She could explode just thinking about it, she says.

"Not here please", I say jokingly and end the preliminary conversation. I can already see the source of her anger, the disturbance in her energy field. She must now lie down on the treatment bench, close her eyes and do absolutely nothing. Nothing at all. She must observe her body, whether it is hot or cold, whether she can feel pressure anywhere; perhaps she thinks thoughts, sees pictures or hears noises. All she has to do is just observe everything, I whisper to her.

This is what the majority of the clients find most difficult. Particularly in our "enlightened" world, we try to solve everything with our head. We are never and can never be quiet. To simply observe ourselves we find very difficult.

We must always do something. And even when we just sit there doing nothing, most of the time we think about our misery. But then our mind is a rather inept instrument. The mind only rarely reaches the deep levels of energies. So thinking is of no use at all, and brooding even less so.

With Franziska I look in the proximity of the solar plexus, the third energy centre (chakra) of the body, and see two or three connections from her energy system to the outside.

Energy flows permanently between humans through connections. Two of the connections I can see are very black, the other one is greyish. From this I can see that nothing good flows between Franziska and the three persons. I sever the connection and observe Franziska. After a few seconds she sighs strongly and murmurs: "… I feel lighter, I feel energy flowing through my body …"

After the session she tells me how she experienced it. Franziska has an excellent memory. What about your resentment, your rage?, I ask her, cutting it short. Franziska's eyes go thoughtful. "It's gone", she says, beaming.

Now you will probably ask yourselves again: What? How can it be so simple? It is not. It's only simple for those who can really "see".

In the course of the afternoon I receive clients with the most diverse issues: anxieties, panics, partner problems, allergies, fear of the future.

'Fear of the future', I think. One can only fear the future if he is not there, where he belongs – when he is a long way away from his destined path, his gifts, his talents. A job we keep just because of the money must make us unhappy in the long run.

Thomas

"A friend told me you hold energetic sessions that can bring destiny back to me", says Thomas, a departmental manager with a telecommunications company. He is the last client today.

"What are you expecting from it?" I ask him.
   "Well, I think that it could be the fastest way to find what makes me happier. My job is not bad, but it's not fulfilling", he continues.
   "What's not fulfilling about it?"
   "The colleagues, but mainly my boss. We don't get along. I think he has something against me. Besides, I feel like the odd one out, a loner, which is certainly not my fault, it's the company", he says to me.

Boss, departmental manager, regional manager – these words bring back old memories, from the days when I worked as an engineer in the industry.

"The people with whom I do this kind of treatment already have a, let's say, certain basic energetic purity."

"Basic purity?", Thomas asks, frowning.

"In a nutshell: you must work on a few introductory issues in order to prepare your energy system to fetch back the future energies."

"Introductory issues?", he asks; he is sceptical.

"Yes, for example your discontent, your rage against your colleagues and your boss… these are issues. It cannot be possible that all of 20,000 employees are bad people. How are things with your friends, with your family? But for now I shouldn't, and may not, say any more. I don't want to prescribe or give you your issues. I'm not allowed to do that – however, this is exactly the work that needs to be done."

Thomas was not prepared to work on these issues on that day, but his rage and discontent would have been a good place to start.

What does all this have to do with our own happy future? What does all this have to do with happiness in life?

Most of my clients or participants in the seminars try to "wish away" problems. The issues are very diverse, for instance: "I would like to live without fear", or "I want to stop thinking about my ex-partner", or "I want to be able to sleep again", or, as in Thomas's case: "I just want to find my destiny and finally attain inner peace."

25

One cannot wish away his problems. It is not possible. It would be like a dentist putting in a crown without removing the caries first. The caries, i.e. the problems, would return, since they have not really been treated.

Only when we really heal our wounds (problems) and turn them into sources of power will we be able to find and live in happiness. There is no other solution. One should take all those out there trying to lead us to believe that there is an easier way, be it mentors, positive thinkers or motivational trainers, with a pinch of salt. Dealing with our past and our experiences is very common in our culture – words like "guilt" or "failure" spring to mind. But one cannot reverse the past.

Shamanism however is part of a different culture. A culture which doesn't rely on cause and effect, which doesn't make destiny conditional upon the past or give everyone a chance that one can totally mess up. This culture doesn't know desires or "goals", to which one is a slave until they are fulfilled. Or even happiness, in the sense that one must attain it. This culture doesn't even like to ask questions. It is the culture of shamans.

El mundo espiritual dos

"Eres mi hermano" was still ringing in my ears. I felt safe inside – no longer alone. And yet a feeling of insecurity often came over me. "Am I energetically infected now?", I would ask myself. Am I dependent on the Q'ero gurus?

I pushed these thoughts aside, and in the following weeks I invited some friends around for healing sessions. At the time,

I wasn't thinking of working as a shaman, but on the other hand I didn't want to waste away my gift. Besides, I wanted to find out whether my healing powers would work in the "real world", and whether I could intentionally switch my "seeing" on and off again.

The first five friends came to me with wholly different problems. They hadn't chosen the worst issues, I noticed – probably because they didn't want me to "look into" their most intimate spheres. On the one hand, that was very moving, but on the other I was annoyed about it.

So I had to deal with backache, breathing problems, itching, sleep disorder and tiredness.

"Oh well", I thought and set out to get rid of energetic swords, objects, black stains and impurities from the luminous energy fields of my friends. The sessions were fun, enormous fun. I really enjoyed them and could hardly wait for the next scheduled appointment.

I asked all of them to come twice and explained that in the first session I would take out the burdensome energy and in the second I would rebalance their energy field. My friends laughed during the sessions – they found it very amusing to be treated by me. They were also very sceptical. They knew I was a good businessman... but a shaman?

Our life contract

Today is Wednesday. The day begins at eight a.m. Of course by now I have assistants who answer the numerous telephone calls. I would much prefer to speak with all callers personally, but there's simply not enough time. The run is too big. Fortunately my assistants can work energetically just as well as I do. This is what is so great about it: anyone can learn it. Some time anyone can heal anyone who needs to be healed. That was the case in former times, and this is my mission, so to speak. Still, I would like to remain accessible for everyone.

In the days when I myself was looking for a solution to my problems, I was often annoyed about not being able to get in touch with the authors of self-help books. It is evidently a fad of German literary figures: publish something, gain a half-god status with the middle-class intellectuals by writing a book, and then be no longer accessible to anyone. Paulo Coelho, who has sold millions of books worldwide, is fantastically reachable through his team. Because of our common interests we are in mail contact. Every single mail I have written to him has been answered. I think this is fair. Everyone has a place in this world, and if they show interest in the meaning of their existence they should be helped.

It really exists, the "meaning of life", a reason why we are in this world. It hasn't just happened. According to many mystery schools, we are all born with a certain life contract. With an energetic life contract, which is embodied deeply inside us, and which will be fulfilled.

I had serious doubts about it. "Destiny": we are not here without a reason, everything is predetermined, the discussions that went on for hours in the religious education class of my youth… all this did not exactly make me very receptive when it came to resurrecting this topic.

Through my work with clients however, this topic came back. In fact, it came through their feedback, hence from their healing process.

Life issues

Each contract is unique to each person. The healthy human intellect as well as the experience from one's own life are proof of that. How many times in our childhood did we try to copy idols and wanted to be as successful as they were? How many adolescents have made a pathetic effort at a keyboard at home, obsessed by the idea of becoming a great musician? But not everyone can be a popstar. And, in adult life: how often do people try to do or copy things that others have gained success with?

Why do most of these attempts fail? Why can't we just copy the happiness of someone else?

For the very simple reason that we must fulfil our own individual life contract. Every one of us. We must find our personal contract, with which we can experience the inner, the real wealth.

Why this contract does not manifest itself in our life is a question which we can answer ourselves. For this we only need to appraise our present quality of life with a critical eye. In order to perceive our life contract by instinct, and thus energetically, which is how it should actually be experienced, we must focus on the four most elementary areas of our life:

Partnership/love, occupation, physical health and mental health.

Now if you take these four areas and answer the question "Am I really unconditionally happy in this area?" sincerely, then you will find how you honestly feel in relation to these areas.

This is nonsense, you will think. No one can be happy without exception in all areas. I say: yes, they can!

Those who live very close to their energetic life contract are happy. They are people who are often looked at with envy by others who are worse off. They are the winners in our society, the people to whom allegedly "everything comes easily".
  But what is this energetic life contract? What does it say?

Also here, this contract is first of all "mere" energy. At the end of the book it will become clearer, of which material the contract consists. Just one thing beforehand: if we can find the contract again and live according to it afterwards, then we will lead a really happy life, a life in paradise.

This is also the reason why we are often dissatisfied. Deep inside us lies dormant a paradisiacal conception of life: our dreams. Dreams which we've all had in our childhood, and which become blunted as we grow older and are destroyed time and again by a sober adjustment to reality. They are the dreams of a better life, of a great love, of fullness and richness in all areas of life.

And this is the reason we keep searching.

We believe that our way of finding these things lies in making exterior changes (in relationship, occupation, residence etc.), in order to feel better inside. Everyone knows that this is a very difficult way, and often what we get in return is exactly the same as what had caused us the trouble before: how often do people change jobs and, after an initial period of excitement, find the new position just as bad as their old one? It is often the same with relationships. We change the partner, but not the energetic pattern. We enter into the next relationship carrying the same problems, often attracting the same type of partner, and after some time we begin to face these problems again. Those who admit this will say: "Fundamentally I was only trying to escape." Because we change something only outwardly, but do not work on the true issue.

What do we escape from?

Every human being has an issue, at least one. It can be physical symptoms such as chronic backache. It could be fears, phobias, envy, sleeplessness, sadness, depressions, diverse symptoms on all levels.

Often they are also flagrant existential things, such as our environment and the circumstances, that can determine our existence. No, not often – always! "The interior manifests itself on the exterior, never the other way round", as Humberto says. We always believe however that we are determined through our environment and from the prevailing factors in it.

The very opposite is the case.

When we change something inside us, when we really heal our wounds, then everything else changes, and that includes our environment. And if we can continue along that path, then we will find our true happiness.

It is the issues that we try to escape from.

Changes don't happen inside our head

In my practice I increasingly came to realize the connection between the intensity of the symptoms and the veering off from one's life path, dreams, vocation, from one's destiny.

In most cases, people who are particularly unwell, both physically and mentally, are those who have a relationship that is no good for them, or a job that makes them unhappy, or live in a place they shouldn't be living in, or do things they shouldn't be doing.

This is logical, everyone would think. And the solution is very simple: we just have to take some steps and change things, change ourselves! We give up smoking, end the relationship, look for another job and simply avoid the things that are not good for us.

The problem is: this is not the way it works. In fact, such decisions work out for maybe a few days or even a couple of weeks at the most, but never in the long run. Only very few can manage to change their inner emotions – and thus their energy – through a conscious decision made in their head.

One of my best friends is one such hardcore case: he decided "in his head" to give up smoking from one day to the next. But although he hasn't smoked since, every time I see him he tells me how much he craves a cigarette. The addiction, and the energy that fuels it, are still there. Evidently, the "head" decision has not healed the addiction, so the craving remains and moves into other areas.

So a decision in the head will not work at all. The root of the evil lies in a deep energetic disturbance. And it is this disturbance that always deals us the same type of partner with whom a relationship will not function, that always puts us next to the type of colleagues who will annoy us. It is this disturbance that always brings the same unhealthy circumstances. Because we basically "attract" what is stored in our energy field, just as a magnet attracts iron filings. It is our untreated deep wounds that keep crying out for manifestation on the exterior. And exactly that prevents us from living our destiny, until we transform the wounds into sources of power – but if we do, our whole life changes. Automatically. And according to the law of resonance, we only attract what is good for us. It's as simple as that.

El mundo espiritual tres

Though none of my friends called, I knew that they would be healed. I knew instinctively that the backaches, breathing problems, itching, sleep disorders and tiredness would disappear.

After I had treated each of them twice I had no more appointments for other sessions.

Four weeks had now passed since the last treatment. No feedback. It can't be, I thought, and had self doubts. That was probably it, I thought at the time. That was the brief history of the healing practice of Martin Brune.

I did not call my friends. I was too scared of failure. Innerly I tried to forget the sessions, and the intensive work with my companies helped me in doing so.

Until, on a Friday, a man called Heiko phoned me.

He was calling me because Uwe had recommended me and given him my number. Uwe had been treated by me because of his backaches, and although he wasn't sure that it was me who'd made the pain go away, his suffering had stopped ever since. They were in the same tennis club, and now he, Heiko, would like an appointment too if possible.

I was speechless. Totally taken aback. Someone was asking for an appointment with Martin Brune, engineer and company owner, to do a healing session. A stranger, of all people?

Happiness finds us

Most of us are classical objectors of destiny. Yet everyone knows their "destiny": deep inside we all have a concrete idea of how we would prefer to live. And there is a simple way to find out:

Close your eyes and ask yourselves how you would like to live if you had the opportunity. Where would it be? Who/which persons would be there with you? Would that be a full life?

How would you live in a relationship? In which city? Which job would fulfil you?

This simple exercise demonstrates the big difference between what we live (reality) and what we see as an ideal. For some of us it can be quite disappointing, because the difference is often enormous. But exactly what we see when we ask ourselves these simple questions is the condition in which we would be at our healthiest and happiest.

Missing our calling and talents in life

When I was twelve, I wanted to study psychology. I thought it would be interesting to work with other people, have deep conversations and be able to help them. In the end however I studied electrical engineering, as, manipulated by my education, I thought security was more important.

There were signs, many of them, that told me not to take the path of security, but I rejected all these generous indications and miracles of life, all the chances, until one day I became very ill.

I was very successful as an entrepreneur and had a very "male" world view, meaning that I felt that men who did yoga were very "shallow" and strange. I was a knight, who bravely continued to ride toward success despite a blood-covered face. Always straight into the lance of the opponent, always ignoring my true talents.

Believe me, I was so far away from my talents and had lost faith in me to such an extent, that never in a lifetime would I have thought that I would work as a shaman one day.

Energy: the path to destiny

In one shape or other, we all come across signs several times during our life. These are often omens. But since we are so extremely driven by our head, we always manage to run away from them.

Literature is teeming with self-realisation books, in which the authors describe the serious illness they have gone through and how they found their vocation through this illness.

In actual fact: do you know someone who, while lying in hospital, has decided to work 60 instead of 50 hours a week in future when he goes back to the office? Those lucky enough to survive a heart attack, for instance, change their life immediately. They realise that old ideals and values suddenly become totally meaningless. These are the famous stories in the style of "the manager who became a farmer".

Therefore, a fundamental change must occur. But in order to find our destiny, we actually don't need to do anything. It finds us, as soon as we are energetically cleansed. One way or another, automatically, everyone. If we don't become "pure", the path to achieve this can be very arduous, painful, or we might set out on it too late or even not at all in this life.

Not everyone must find his or her destiny like I did, through a serious illness. There are tools and techniques which we can learn in order to find our destiny without having to go through a serious illness AND in this life. The old mystery schools possessed this knowledge. In the Energy School students learn energetic techniques that help them discover and also experience "destiny" – in this life. In the Envisioning course one learns to "manifest" his/her dreams, and thus fulfil them in real life. And, trust me, it could turn out that the reason for your existence on earth can be a lot more than your nameplate on your desk.

El mundo espiritual quatro

Heiko's "issues" were also healed, and he recommended me to about ten new clients. Word of my treatment seemed to get around. But I still felt a little uneasy. During that time every action I undertook in the energy field of a client caused an immediate reaction. I was learning. I was learning more with each client, and I felt like a magician who could move between worlds. Energetic swords were pulled out, and the backache disappeared. Iron balls were removed, and the gastritis was gone. Glass splinters were extracted, and the asthma vanished.

I had no one with whom I could talk about it. I was all alone with this. As far as I knew there was no one else in Germany who worked in the same way. I was fighting not only against the dark light of the clients, but also against myself. Against my own scepticism. It was a time when I too underwent radical changes.

After about three months the weekends weren't enough anymore. I had to add Friday as a day for treatment. I decided to take clients every other Friday – that could be arranged with the other work I had to do in my companies.

"A shaman is an intermediary between worlds", I read in a book once. An intermediary between the real, manifested world and the invisible world of spirits and energy.

That's exactly how I felt. As a warrior of the light, who could relieve illness by pulling out energetic symbols and objects. And I gradually got better.

ENERGY, IMBALANCE, HEALING and CONNECTING

What is energy?

 S o what stops us from living our happiness – and I mean here and now and not at some time in the distant future? The answer is very simple: it is the energetic stains, the internal dramas, the experiences from our past in this and in previous lives, which always look for new manifestation in our everyday life. If we are energetically pure, then we live in our destiny. Because then we only attract "pure things".

A picture analogous to our life is that of a river, which has its source somewhere in the mountains; at first the river flows, then it comes across the first obstacles, the first big boulders, which change the river's course so that the river floods large areas and does not reach the sea (the destiny). This is a way of describing the energy balance, and thus in a transferred sense the life of a human being.

What energy medicine does is simply remove the boulders, the impurities in our energy system.

This does not happen in a lengthy, psychoanalytical process, neither does it involve physical work or drugs. It happens very fast: with the aid of the seeing abilities of a shaman, a spiritual doctor, who just clears away these boulders in a few simple treatment sessions, and just eliminates the shadows in one's energy field.

The emphasis here lies on "fast" and "simple". All the students who attend the Foundation course of the Energy School for the first time share the same enthusiasm about how quickly even the most serious problems can disappear within a few minutes.

In my Energy School I have given this procedure the name "clearing process"; it is the "wiping out" of black stains, of traumas in our luminous energy field.

Body, soul, mind, and ... energy

Everyone knows that there are different levels on which we are engaged in the world. We classify these into the categories body, soul and mind. Simply put, the condition of a human being can be "divided" into and described by these three constituents. Everyone takes into account these three conditions. When we ask ourselves how we feel at any given moment, then we "enquire" with these three constituents and obtain a result. For instance: my body feels tired (body), I feel frustrated (soul), I am thinking about it (mind).

There is however a constituent that has been forgotten, and this is energy. Moreover, it is exactly this part that is the root of all evil in the river of life. It is not the body, not the mind, and not the soul, but an "imbalance" of energy which causes us to think about a symptom (mind), experience an indisposition (mentally), and feel an illness (physically).

To clarify this once again: the reason for a physical problem is not the body. The reason for a mental, psychological problem is not the soul. The reason for eternal brooding is not the mind. The reason always lies in a disturbance of our energy.

So what is this energy, about which all spiritual schools, yoga trends, energy and mystery schools tell us? How can we envisage energy? Before we talk about "light", we should perhaps start with the dark energies, the energy disturbances: the "black stains".

El mundo espiritual cinco

Despite the increasing number of treatments – meanwhile I was having sessions on all evenings of the week – I was still feeling very uncertain and lonely with all of this.

There was no one here with whom I could talk about it. Don Humberto and the other shamans were a long way away and unreachable by telephone. I believed in what I was doing, but I still had doubts, and there was no one around who could take them away for me.

These doubts only had to do with myself. A latent fear was lurking that I might lose my grip one day and go totally insane.

A flood of images. I had now done 200 consultations. I was receiving so much feedback from successful healings that it would make your hair stand on end. Allergies disappeared, asthmas vanished, no more nightmares, no fear of the future, fear of flying disappeared, long mails were received about positive changes in the circumstances of my clients. Over 150 mails about improvements, enormous steps forward that clients had made, and everywhere at the bottom "thank you, Martin".

Yet my self-doubts remained. For heaven's sake, I thought to myself, everyone here says that what you do has a positive effect.

It was one Sunday in spring, I lit a few tea lights and closed my eyes. It is very quiet here, I thought. Unusually quiet for a city. It was dark. Sometimes it does us good just to close our eyes. I remembered a gesture Don Francisco made when I was leaving. He pointed up to the sky and said something like: "Hatun Chasca" – and he said it several times. "Hatun Chasca" – or something similar.

In my mind I saw Don Francisco, or rather his index finger, pointing to the sky. I saw a ray of light that shone through the ceiling, through the roof of the house, past the trees, into the sky, through the clouds, and reached the stars. I followed this ray of light that seemed to have no end, through the stars, past the moon, further and further away.

I opened my eyes. The treatment room was dark. The neighbours across the street were cooking, I saw. I closed my eyes again. The journey of the light continued. Until it reached a door, a door made of light. What on earth was that? I didn't get any further. The ray of light seemed to end here.

"It's all in your mind; you've always had a wild imagination, ever since you were a child", I thought. I opened my eyes and made myself some tea.

Chakras and black stains

What happens now in these energy fields?

According to the views of many mystery schools, including that of the Incas, what holds the knowledge of both our physical and mental problems is not our memory or our body, but the luminous body. This is new, but at the same time old. This knowledge was part of our culture 5,000 years ago – but it has fallen into oblivion. Today we think that every trauma, every memory will be stored in our brain and thus in our head.

However, a human being consists not only of a physical body, but also of an energetic, a luminous body. This luminous body consists roughly of nine sections, or energy centres, that are called chakras (the word "chakra" comes from Sanskrit and means "spinning wheel").

Let's take a psychoanalytical treatment by an analyst, such as I have experienced hundreds of times. The session usually begins with the analyst asking how we are. Let's assume we don't feel so well physically at that moment, maybe we feel weak, and our motivation is also at a low ebb. The analyst then notices that the association of "physical weakness" and "low motivation" has already existed before at a certain point, and goes into this specific situation in our life. And all of a sudden, we find ourselves dealing with an issue from the past during treatment. We talk about it, old feelings come up, and the physical pain intensifies, or maybe subsides for a while.

Of course, this is a rather simplified example, but it demonstrates that, during such therapies, we move through the three levels: body, soul, and mind. Therapies can sometimes go on for many years without finding the true source of the problem: the energy imbalance. The true source of the problem lies in the luminous energy field of the client – in the individual chakras. The traumas and illnesses can basically be found in the luminous field of the client, which envelops the physical body. Dark stains are, simply put, the traumas, the energy disturbances which release a symptom, either mental, or physical, or both. Once all these stains have been removed, the chakra is "clean" and the client/patient has no symptoms – he is healthy.

Energy is also information.

But what is in a black stain?

First of all, it is information that is embedded in a black stain, also in the form of energy. Going back to the story of Elenor at the beginning of this book, the entire scenery, consisting of the condor, the landscape, the woman, the boat and the burning house are embedded in it. Not only the images are in this black stain, i.e. in the energy disturbance, but also the drama, the fears, the suffering, and the coldness of the image. The drama of these images, which are the emotions lying "beneath" the images, is actually what the client feels in "real" life. This means that the energy disturbance, the black stain, has at some point in the past penetrated into our energy field and permanently informs our entire perceptual mechanisms: the levels of the soul, the mind, and the body.

When we, in real life, feel fear in certain situations, then our mind already makes the first mistake: we think that the situation is the cause of the fear. But the situation has basically only activated a black stain in our energy field – with all its emotions, with all its drama.

The situation is therefore only the trigger for something which lies dormant deep inside us as an energy disturbance.

The students at my Energy School who learn to "see" the energies, can actually see the history that is behind such a stain. They can see and decode the energy of the pollution, of the black stain.

As soon as a stain has become visible, a shaman can easily take it away. This is achieved with intent. The shaman "extracts" with his intent the black stain from the chakra, i.e. from the luminous body of the client, and the symptom disappears, as the source of the energy disturbance has been removed.

What takes the place of the black stain is light. Pure, clean light. Simple, isn't it? You don't believe me at all, do you? I admit that we are used to having to work on everything, and that at the bottom of everything there always must be an achievement. Everyone has heard of book titles such as "Illness as a way forward", "What my illness has taught me" or similar, but: nature does not intend a complicated healing procedure! Healing can happen unbelievably fast. This is my experience day after day in my practice and at my Institute.

When you cut your finger while doing something, have you ever observed how long it lasts until the blood clots and a scab is formed? Three hours, two hours, one hour, twenty minutes, five minutes, one minute? Probably not even thirty seconds. And that is the same with all wounds, irrespective of whether they are mental or physical. It depends on the size of the wound, some will say: Yes, it's true… but the bigger the wound, the bigger the energy disturbance the wound is based on. And when this disturbance disappears, then even the worst symptoms will disappear.

Don Humberto always used to say: "Martin, if a snake bites you, you go to a doctor. He will bandage your hand, put iodine on the wound and prescribe some drugs. If, however, you want to know WHY the snake bit you, then go to a shaman."

Are you afraid of snakes? Or, are you afraid of anything at all? Maybe of saying "no"? Or of the dark, the night, or of the future? Heal your fears, because they are only waiting to be substantiated. Luckily there are no snakes in our latitude, otherwise those who fear them would attract them as if by magic.

El mundo espiritual seis

Although I knew I was just fantasizing, I closed my eyes and travelled again along the ray of light to the stars, past the moon, to the door, and tried to open it.

The door consisted of light. Pure light. I had never seen anything so incredibly large. To the left and right of the door stood enormous trees and plants which enshrouded an un-believable wall of light. Everything consisted of light. Sometimes the light was greenish, other times it was bright, or a little darker, just bright enough that I could make out the plants, the trees, the stones, the wall and the door. Nothing was really transparent; I could not look through. Yet the objects were not solid either, as they would be in our world. The light was different up there. It was more beautiful. It felt better. It was warm.

Curious as I was, I tried to push the door open. But it wouldn't open, I simply could not open it. "Llamas al espírtu y el espíritu responde, el espíritu te llama y tu respondes". "You call the spirit, and the spirit answers. The spirit calls you, and you answer." This occurred to me suddenly.

So I asked for help. I no longer know how I did it, but I asked for someone to come and help me, to let me in. And then something mobile appeared, a kind of ghost – and it had the face of Don Humberto.

"Always ask for the spirit's permission", he said when he saw me, and finally opened the door. "Always ask for permission". That was obviously the first lesson I had to learn.

Healing between worlds

Therefore we must go to a shaman if, rather than remove the symptoms (the snake bite), we want to remove the causes (black stains, why the snake bit us). We go to a "magician between worlds". The shaman or energy healer is a master in moving between the world of the body, the soul, and the mind and the invisible world, the world of energy. This invisible world presents itself to the shaman in very absurd images,

47

as you will remember from the example of the very novel-like and mystical description recounted in the opening story.

Let's go back to our different perceptual mechanisms and the levels of body, soul, and mind. These are now completed with the addition of the level of energy.

The healing process is enabled through these levels: a change at the source, at the energy level, i.e. the removal of the black stains, informs the soul level, the soul level in turn informs the mental level, and the mental level then informs the physical. Therefore symptoms such as fear of flight (soul) can disappear completely after just one session, but a severe backache (body) may take a week. This happens because the change of energy, which is the source of the backache, must first be "communicated" to the soul, then to the mind and finally to the body.

It can therefore take some time before the healed energy is passed to and manifested in the other three levels, and thus before the disappearance of the symptom becomes evident and, more importantly, "felt".

The shaman moves between the world of body, soul and mind, and the world of energy.

In order to understand the simplicity of this medicine we must only learn and accept that the source of our problems is always an energy disturbance and that the world of energy does exist! However, energy disturbances cannot be removed by using our head/mind.

Elka

Today I have ten sessions. Elka came at five o'clock in the afternoon. She says she would like to know what her mission in life was. Her issue: the constant nervousness that accompanies her; also, she assumes that something must have happened in her family tree with her grandmother, and that is the reason why she has such problems. She has never had contact with her grandmother – and she would wish that she could be able to establish contact with her and could she learn to do that…

"Phew! That's a lot!", I say. "Things are getting mixed up here. First of all you should know that your mission, or your destiny, will actually find you automatically when the energy can flow freely. What stops us from identifying our destiny is our energetic contamination. You can learn to speak with your deceased grandmother. One can learn to develop contact with ancestors. I could speak for you with the spirit of your grandmother, but the knowledge about what happened at some point decades ago will not help you to heal. What is important, and what we have to look into, is what your search for a mission does to you. I mean, where does the desire to know your destiny come from? Uncertainty in life? What does your life do to you at the moment? How do you feel?"
"Sad. Life makes me sad", says Elka.

Elka comes with an issue, for which, like every so often, she has a cognitive solution on hand. The cognitive solution however, which is based on the mechanism of the mind, does not change the basic emotion of sadness. Her soul says to her that she must know her mission, or destiny, and then she would feel better. Her mind even advices her to look more into her past (grandmother) and ponder over it – because if she knew what happened at that time, she could then solve her problem.

With this example, we can see how intricately the mind works: it constructs something "round about", in order to change the basic sense of melancholy that one feels.

Many people want to change their lives but start in the wrong place.

Many change the external circumstances, move from one place to the next, change their jobs, or change their partners. But the problems or the pain remain.
Sadness is what the shaman works with, because sadness, a deep feeling, is closer to the level of energy. Sadness is the issue, not the search for a mission, not the past of the grandmother. Sadness is basically the springboard, from which the healer or shaman "jumps" into the invisible world of energy to explore which energy disturbance produces this feeling.

The process is always to transform the wound, in this case sadness, into a source of power. When the sadness (dark energy) is eliminated, only cheerfulness (luminous energy, bright light) can take its place. So the task consists of looking deeply into the wounds and transforming them. Yet this is a task that takes a lot of courage, because we must "look" directly into the problem, no matter how much it scares us.

Uwe

Uwe has a purely physical problem, he says. His knees ache, particularly in the morning.

"Do you have a, let's say, superordinate idea about your knee problem?", I ask.

"Superordinate?", Uwe asks, frowning.

"Yes, it could be that you are under a lot of stress… or at least have the feeling…"

"One is always under stress, no?", says Uwe defensively.

We see that stress is normal for Uwe, but physical symptoms aren't. His example shows how separate from ourselves we can live.

During the introductory discussion I often lead the client from a pure physical issue, from the body level, to the notion of a somewhat deeper level. For the physical symptom is always a manifestation of energy imbalance in deeper levels. An aching knee can have as its source a relationship problem that was repressed long ago. Because the source of ALL symptoms is the imbalance of energy.

I cannot repeat this often enough: the reason for a physical problem is not the body. The reason for a mental, psychological problem is not the soul. The reason for eternal brooding is not the mind. The reason can always be found in a disturbance, an imbalance, of our energy.

For that reason the illness is not important to the shaman, because after all the illness is only a consequence of the energy disturbance and the "entry point", from which the shaman commences the journey to the levels of energy.

Franka

It is Monday, eleven a.m. Franka from Vienna calls me for a long-distance treatment.

„I am very excited!", she says.

„This is normal! Most of the people who come to me for the first time are, because this type of treatment is new", I say.

„Yes, but my case is particularly bad. I just don't know who I am."

„I see, that's the reason you're calling. What exactly do you mean by that?"

"Well, I have changed jobs over 30 times in my life. One job was worse than the other, and at the moment I'm unemployed again. It's not that there are no jobs in Vienna, but I always feel unhappy with these jobs.

Before, I had dreams and visions about what I wanted to do with my life, but now even that is gone. No more dreams – no more visions. I always thought it was normal, but what is normal in the end? I assume that other people are better off in this way. Right now I feel crazy. I'm somewhere in the middle, and..."

"Stop, Franka, stop, this is all too fast... tell me, how does all that affect you? I mean, how do you feel about it? Maybe under pressure, helpless, depressed?"

"How do I feel about it...", she repeats. She is quiet and thinks for a while. Then she says: "Nothing!"

„How do you mean, nothing?", I ask.

„You see, this is another one of my problems... I just don't feel anything. I can't even do that...", she says.

"Ok, but don't you feel anything physical?", I ask, virtually begging for symptoms.

"Physical? Yes, I have problems with my stomach, I often suffer from headaches, and I have an ache in my chest, but that's been there for a long time", she lists her ailments.

During the course of the treatment we found a deep sadness,

connected to a fear of failure in life, to be the actual reason for her constant job changing. When the responsibilities became greater, she fled from them.

It is always interesting to see the edifice of thoughts our mind produces in order to analyse and "fix" the reason for our problems: in most cases our misery is the fault of other people. Sometimes it is our partner, or our mother, father, our colleagues, the circumstances, the house, the children, or shortage of money.

With my energetic work over time, I have come to the conclusion that roughly 90 percent of all the theories about the "why" are wrong. As I've already mentioned at the beginning, our mind is rather an inept instrument for solving emotional, mental or physical problems.

Thinking is not the solution.

Can we heal ourselves?

This is the most frequently asked question at my seminars. Yes, we can. It really is possible. Then why is it not so simple? Why can we not just lie down, give the instruction "self-heal" or, better, "please heal me!" and simply wait to be healed?

The reason is very simple: the average human being is not able to reach into the depths of his own heavy energy disturbances in order to set them free. That is the only reason.

I am aware of the contemporary trend towards self-healing; but I can also see that it suits more our ideal western self-perception of doing everything alone without any help from others.

There are numerous writers who propagate self-healing in their books. All these authors have one thing in common: they have gone through a serious illness, and the techniques they have developed in order to master their illness are now supposed to help others.

Yet other people are not as seriously ill as these authors, who were on the brink of death. In the end, these authors had no choice but probing very deep into their own energy disturbance in order to finally set it free – and this is what saved their life. Average human beings, at least those who are not about to die, will be too scared to encounter the darkness deep inside themselves.

It is not necessary for each client to go through a heavy process. The shaman can, instead of the client, look into his/her dark energy disturbances and remove them, without the client having to experience or even "re-experience" the pain.

Another reason why self-healing can be difficult is that we often don't know or cannot accurately identify where the problem lies. Most clients come with a rather spongelike feeling, with a "mash" of many symptoms at the same time. This is the reality. Where are we supposed to start with our self-healing?

At first, a shaman helps to remove the largest rocks from the river of our life. I do not want to belittle the works of other authors, their work is wonderful, but if you can make no progress, then do not give up! Use someone else to help! Once a certain degree of purity has been reached in your energy system, then you can still think about self-healing the distressing symptoms that remain.

El mundo espiritual siete

"Always ask for permission": I had understood this lesson. The door of light opened and I saw a large, a very large room. Its walls were decorated with beautiful stones. They looked like crystals. At first I thought it was a church, but then it was just a room again with lovely wall decorations made of stones.

The spirit led me across the room to a table, which was bathed in a beautiful, warm light. There were no lights or candles to be seen. The light was just there, enveloping this table – it turned it into a table of light.

"What is your name?", I asked the spirit.

"Today it is Mavelino", said the spirit.

"Why today – what will you be called tomorrow?"

"I have a thousand names, for the entire knowledge of the universe is shared out among an infinite number of spirits", said the spirit.

I opened my eyes and looked at the dark Cologne night through the window of the practice. There was no spirit to be seen – only a few lights in the windows of the houses opposite. I rubbed my eyelids, wanting to make sure I wasn't dreaming it all, and closed my eyes again.

This time I was no longer an observer of the room: I was in it and the spirit was right in front of me! I broke out in a cold sweat. I opened my eyes. The consultation room, the neighbours, everything was in order. I closed my eyes again and saw the spirit standing in front of the table.

"Why you are here now, Mavelino? Why am I in this room?", I asked the spirit. "I am here because you need some answers right now, and I can give you these answers. On another day it may be that you need different answers, then another spirit will come. From me you will learn how to become a good shaman", he answered.

"Oh, a good shaman… But I'm scared that when I close my eyes to go to sleep I will always see this room, that I won't be able to switch off. I don't want to go mad with all this hocus-pocus here." Mavelino came closer and blew on me. I shivered, and my fear disappeared.

I opened my eyes. Someone across the road was cooking. I felt a hot burning sensation on my chest. "Martin, you must always keep this to yourself", I thought to myself. "You are not some kind of weird esoteric type", and imagined my friends smiling with pity or laughing at me.

"Then just go back through the door and travel along the ray of light back to your world. If you want to come again, you know how it works. Always ask for permission, whatever you do. I am very, very patient. I have been here for centuries, so two or three days will not make any difference. You should know that we have no linearity here, no 'time'. And by the way... may I introduce Daph to you, a wonderful shaman from our fifth world – the world of the spirits. She and I will support you with your healings in future."

Daph was striking. I had never seen such a beautiful woman before. She moved like a girl, had the hands of a mother, and bright hair of light that almost touched the ground. She was stunningly beautiful.

"What a load of rubbish", I thought. "This is total projection – this is the kind of woman you wish as a partner". I laughed at my own naïvety, opened my eyes, packed my things, left the practice, drove home and went to bed.

I closed my eyes but couldn't sleep; suddenly I was lying in this room. Mavelino was staring at me as though I was being counted out in a boxfight. Now it's happened. Now I've finally cracked up. It doesn't matter anymore.

"Mavelino, what is this?", I looked at the spirit questioningly, and I felt like Don Camillo (from the movie "The Little World of Don Camillo"), when he speaks with God. 'Luckily nobody here can hear me speak', I thought.

"You ask the spirit, and the spirit answers – it's as simple as that", he said.

"But how can I switch off what I'm seeing here? I want to sleep!"

"Travel back to your world – and for heaven's sake: don't ask so many questions." This last sentence I remembered from the Q'ero. They didn't like questions either.

I did as he told me, and travelled back through the door, past the moon and the stars, through the clouds, back to this earth, back here to my apartment. Had I found new teachers and helpers? "Virtual teachers", so to speak?

I will not tell any of this to anyone, I thought. No one would believe me. First I surprise all my friends by starting to work as a shaman, then I have overwhelming success with it, and now I am in contact with spirits? That takes the biscuit!

No one needs to know this, I thought. The clients are only interested in being healed. "No hocus-pocus", a friend had said once. How the healing comes about doesn't matter to them. It doesn't matter, I thought, this is the right attitude.

"You ask the spirit, and the spirit answers": all right. I had learned something again.

Forms of energy

Monday, nine in the morning. I must read through 103 emails. My co-author has written again: "Martin, you write so much about energy, this is very woolly to the reader – what is this energy – how can one imagine it? A little more please…"

"A little more please", lingers in my mind. How am I supposed to describe energies? "A little more please": that's what they're like, the intellectuals. I never wanted to write a book about it. Books consist of words. Words belong to the mind level.

Energy medicine has nothing to do with the mind – one can only "experience" it. This desire to always want to "understand" everything makes me mad. "Wanting to understand everything" actually means seeking security – a very western, energy-draining approach. Nonetheless one does not find security through words, but only by feeling it, experiencing it.

Most students in the Foundation course are surprised by the fact that I often answer their questions in brief or sometimes even return the question. The reason is that most questions we ask others have only one purpose: to find "security" in the shape of the life energy of another person. Often we ask for fear of doing something wrong; we want assurance. What most people don't seem to notice is that most questions already contain the accurate answer.

In my Energy School there are no manuscripts – we only hand out few "papers". The knowledge of healing, and what it is about, is a knowledge that is passed on purely verbally. Our course consists of practical exercises at a ratio of around eighty percent. It is about experiencing how symptoms disappear: fear of the future, the fear of flying, tinnitus, backaches, the nightmares. Then usually the questions also stop coming, and the doubts disperse. The mind is turned off, and one arrives into the liberating state of "simply acting".

Everyone can see "energy" – we just don't know how. One hundred percent (!) of all students who do the Seeing course can see energy.

So what are energies?

When, for instance, we ask someone we pass how he is, in most cases he will say: "Fine, thanks for asking", and will ask us back how we are. "Very well, thanks", we will reply. After this exchange we go our separate ways. Perhaps in the evening, when we are back home, we might think of this person and realise that he probably didn't really mean the "Fine, thank you" he said. We have the impression that he didn't feel so fine. Perhaps we also have a distorted picture of him in our head, in which he looks almost as if he is about to cry, or even crying. And that basically means that we can see "energy" – the true face behind the mask.

In the Energy School the students learn to see the real, the energetic picture of the client and how to heal it.

Minor energies

Minor energies are energies which enter us briefly and are exuded again by the normal energetic motion of the luminous body, just like respiration. There are hundreds of situations, in which minor energies enter us from the "outside" but do not settle inside us. An example could be a brief, annoyed discussion about overcrowded trains with the conductor, which is usually forgotten after a few minutes.

Children are usually energetically very pure at birth. Ask

a small child one hour after he's had a tantrum what the tantrum was about. In most cases he will probably not even remember it. That is because the energy system of a child is usually less polluted and pure like a crystal. By breathing, which causes a higher and faster vibration of the chakras, the less-dense energies are simply expelled from the luminous body again: everything is forgotten. Adults, on the other hand, dwell on things, become upset and often furious, trapped in their own memory. The energetic memory, which is the number of black stains, increases with age unless it becomes cleansed.

Imagine that you could forget as quickly as children do. Life would be a delight, every day would be a new day. So in order to become strong and healthy again, we must become pure like a crystal, like a child.

Heavy energies

Manuela has constant backache. She has been suffering since her teenage years, she says. At the age of 15 she was in a traffic accident. The pain cannot be seen from the outside, and X-rays furnish no further information as to where this pain comes from.

I look at Manuela's luminous energy field and discover an enormous metal bar (of course in a purely energetic sense, as an image) from her neck down to the buttocks. I carefully pull the bar out, Manuela's body "twitches" a little, and she begins to weep. After the session Manuela feels a lot lighter; she can still feel the pain, but it is already much more bearable, she says.

Many clients who have suffered accidents come to me because they are still in pain. Physically, everything has healed, the doctors can find no symptoms. In most cases the reason is an energy, which still "sits" in the luminous energy field and manifests itself as pain. Such an energy can enter into the luminous body through an impact of an accident and settle there. Then the energetic wound is not yet closed. I've had clients who have still had pains from an accident which took place over 30 years ago.

These heavy, or dense, energies are formed in the human energy body over the years as a result of a life in energetic environments such as family, school, job; factors from which we cannot flee so easily.

A child growing up in problematic family conditions will have dark energy stains in his luminous body from a young age. These stains will persistently seek repetition of these experiences on the exterior.

That is because of the law of resonance, which I will explain later in the book. It is because we can only live on the exterior what is energetically stored in our luminous body.

The energetic drama continues at school. If energetic stains already exist in the luminous field, then, during the school years, these stains look for manifestation in the real world as traumas. In addition, a child may have schoolmates he cannot stand. He doesn't really get on with anyone. He becomes an outsider and doesn't know why.

Did you have an easy childhood?

What do you think would happen in the life of a client if one could erase the childhood stains, these heavy energies?

The root of the evil is the energetic disturbance and not the childhood memories, which must be reappraised laboriously.

In the Seeing course of the Energy School the students learn to remove the energetic connections to our parents. Ninety percent of all humans are not free; they are still moulded by their parents' dramas and relive these. Ninety percent of all humans have "open" issues with their mother or father – even when they are long deceased. In the Seeing course tools are offered to dissolve, to terminate these issues. There exist many different types of therapies, and they offer important insights into the family drama, but in our school we deal with the energetic solution to the issue. Students report of an enormous energy impetus after "stripping off" this heavy burden from their past.

In shamanic tradition children are "energetically" separated from their parents at an early age and connected with "Mother Earth" and "Father Moon". In this way one leaves the guidance of his/her life in the care of these "new" parents, who are always by our side and lead us with their warmth. This too happens during the Seeing course.

Energies and death – spirit possessions

Very few people know that, at the moment of death, the luminous energy field stays on the body of the deceased person for about another 24 hours, and only then does it slowly become detached from the physical body.

At the moment of death most people, predominantly out of fear, decide not to depart from this world because essential things are still missing from their life or are incomplete. Only few have found their destiny in life, and the fear of death, the fear of the unexpected, is the greatest fear of all.

It is the apologies one has never offered, the "I love you"s never told, the still open conflicts between us and our friends, brother, sister, father, or mother. Often it is the never expressed "thanks for everything" that still want to be voiced.

At the moment of death time is limited. Most people do not die surrounded by their family or among their close friends, as is often the case in films.

Everyone who doesn't know how dying really is is very frightened of death. But which living human being could possibly know what dying is like?

Not many people have real company when they die; in most cases they are not let go by those closest to them.

The fear of death and the panic of that moment, together with the desire to live on, cause the luminous body, the energy field, to be transferred into another living energy field.

The physical body dies, but the luminous body of the dying person lives on in another body. Those dying mostly select a person themselves, a person to whom they had a great connection and openness in life and energetically merge with this body.

I admit that this sounds quite eerie. We should not imagine that a whole human being turns into another. What does pass on is the energy of a dying person: all their traumas, qualities and characteristics. Their energy "continues to live" in somebody else, in an attempt to fulfil their life contract, to find their destiny through the new host.

In the Healing School students learn to bring these energies out into the light. They learn to speak with occupiers, ask them where they come from, what they died of, under what circumstances. After these psychodramas, the energies usually consent to be led to the light. Quite a few of these energies are hundreds of years old and still inform our everyday life.

El mundo espiritual ocho

After my experience with the spirits I was no longer working alone. While before it happened I had always worked directly on the light field of the clients, now, at the beginning of the treatment, I saw the energy field of the client but also the room, decorated with gold and jewels, and the beautiful marble light table. The client lay energetically on this table.

The two healing spirits would sit one or two metres away. They had different names and looked different every time, as each client was different and had different issues.

It occurred to me that the shamanic way is one of abundance. The assistance upon which we can fall back is gigantic. Different spirits appear for each client, different specialists with new knowledge.

I was able to ask the spirits. And they answered. They were like very experienced doctors, like highly skilled energy surgeons, who trained me, instructed me and sharpened my awareness.

But apart from teaching me, their "main job" was to work with me, so that in principle there were three of us doing the treatment: the feminine spirit, the masculine spirit and myself.

They would instruct me what to do; the smallest deviations from their instructions were met with criticism, which was expressed immediately in the form of signs. The warning raised index finger of the spirits during treatment is embedded in my memory.

The spirits taught me to give up my ego trip. At first I thought it was me doing the healing. My ego was strengthened and flattered from the clients' positive feedback. I was like an artist who always wants to hear how wonderful his paintings are.

Gradually the spirits taught me that the actual healer wasn't me but the spirits themselves. I was merely a tool – a "medium", according to esoteric terminology.

The treatments became increasingly effective and faster –better and better. The clients would come to me with their issues, and the spirits would tell me in fractions of a second in which energy centre (chakra) the illness or the problem was to be found. I would then move into this chakra, look at the "real" story "behind" the illness and perform the energetic healing.

The real energetic stories I could see increasingly took the shape of mystical animated cartoons. In the second chakra of one client, I saw her energy tied to a steel chain by a man in uniform – she always got involved with dominant types of men. With someone else, I saw in his fourth chakra that he was flying over a landscape on fire – he was suffering from difficulty in breathing, constant panic and tinnitus. With yet another client, I saw in his third chakra his energy trapped inside a gas lamp which was buried in a shelter deep under the ground – this client had asthma and agoraphobia. Another time I saw in someone's first chakra his energy jammed in a cage surrounded by poisonous water – the client was suffering from permanent backache and felt often tired and listless.

"What am I supposed to do with these symbolic mystic stories?", I asked the spirits.

"They are just images, Martin, nothing more. They are the renditions of energy into images – nothing more than that", was the answer I was given.

"But what is the point of these stories – if one cannot change them?"

"We can change the stories. Remember that you are in a chakra, and that every living creature consists of energy. Think about how it should be!"

"How it should be? Am I to simply remove the darkness, the poison from the chakras and transform them into light?"

"Stop asking so many questions, just do it", said Helena, and Morales nodded approvingly. These were the names of the healing spirits today.

"Yes, but how?", I asked.

Energetic connections

When the Q'ero came to Europe, we told them about the new technologies, like e-mail, that help us to communicate with one another. They laughed and said to me: "Martin, we are all connected to each other – even without e-mail."

The old medicine men and women don't talk much; but such sentences make an indelible impression and stay in one's memory forever.

At first I had not understood exactly what that meant. In my seminars I always tell the example of our best friend who calls at the very instant we are thinking of him/her. Strictly speaking we don't need to talk on the phone any-more when we want to find out how to other person is. As soon as we think of this person, we basically "enquire" with the emotional state of him/her over the distance and know how they are!

Only those who live in total separation and are cut off from their own intuition might have trouble sensing it. But these energetic connections are a lot more than that, as I was able to experience later.

Babette

I worked with Babette for the first time. She travelled from Spain, because she had attended one of my seminars in Barcelona.

Babette could not describe her problem. She was actually doing really well; she had a great husband and two children, and had recently moved back home to Barcelona from Italy. Soon she would begin to paint again, do something for herself.

Nonetheless she often felt terrible; it was like a feeling of heaviness, she said, as if something was pulling her down. And then there was this sadness, an incredible sadness that would sometimes come over her without warning. She couldn't say where this weariness came from, she said. In any case this definitely had nothing to do with her life, seeing as everything in it was all right.

After she had been lying on the treatment table for a short while, I was able to identify the cause of her issue: going out from her third chakra, which is the solar plexus, she had a connection that looked like a cord. This cord went out from her luminous body, across the treatment room and out through the window like a hose.

"It would be interesting to find out where the connection goes to", I thought and looked as if by coincidence at a globe I had in my practice.

I imagined the map of Germany and saw the connection stretching from Cologne, past the border and across France to Spain. To the north of Spain.
   "Your fantasy is getting the better of you again", I joked with myself.

"Northern Spain", I thought. It can't be right. She said she was from Barcelona. But somehow I saw the connection ending in Andorra.

I've never had anything like this before, I thought. Have I gained a new ability? I went to the end of the connection and saw the energy, or rather the energetic image of a woman, perhaps in her late sixties. She did not seem happy.

Amazing, I thought, but I did not dare to ask Babette.
    "I see an energy, a feminine energy", I said carefully.
    "Feminine? It must be me", said Babette.
    "No, I mean a connection to a feminine energy in Spain", I tried again.
    "Feminine energy in Spain? It is my mother! My mother!", she said.

Bull's-eye, I thought. Now if I also get right that she doesn't live in Barcelona but in Andorra, then I've got another thing that I cannot tell anyone about because they'll think I'm crazy.

"Tell me, your mother doesn't live in Barcelona, does she?"
    "In Barcelona? No... she lives further north..."
    A cold shiver went down my spine – I felt like a tracker dog, able to track down the prey from miles away.

"Maybe in Andorra?", I asked with a shaky voice.
    "Andorra?", "No, no, she doesn't live in Andorra – she lives in the Basque country."
    "Oh really?", I said. Damn, it would have been too good to be true, I thought. It would have been sensational.
    During the session I cut off the connection and cleaned her third chakra. Babette felt better at once. She admitted that

she was thinking of her mother often, and said that when she heard that a connection to her existed, it became clear to her that the sadness was not at all hers, but that of her mother. This energy, the weariness of her mother, was permanently "flowing" into her.

Many clients describe this effect as a feeling of permanently being "sucked out". This can be coming from the partner, a friend, or the children. With healthy human beings this connection is separated automatically.

A few weeks later Babette sent me an e-mail, in which she wrote that she was feeling extremely well. Her mother had phoned a lot more often since, as though she had noticed that the connection had been separated, but Babette said she had nothing more to give her. Now her mother was looking for a therapist.

Great, I thought. When such connections are cut off, then the healing doesn't only include those who came to see me, but also those to whom the connection existed.

With many clients I still see connections to ex-partners, to relationships that have been over for many years. Most of them are in a new relationship, but the energy still seems to flow into the old relationship. This is also the reason why a separation is not necessarily complete when a couple move apart. Everyone knows that. One of them could move as far away as Toronto, but the energetic connection remains until it is cut off. The separation from a partner can happen a lot faster and, more importantly, less painfully, if these connections are energetically separated.

Weeks had passed since I had first identified and separated connections. My daughter was in the practice with me, playing with the globe.

I could see Spain on it. I thought of Babette again and looked at the northern part, and I couldn't believe it: it wasn't Andorra, of course, that lay in the northernmost of Spain – it was the Basque country. I had got the countries mixed up. I had been exactly right. I had really seen that her mother lived in the Basque country – which I had thought was Andorra...

„Yehhhhhiiiiiiiiiiiiiiiiiiyooooooooooooooooo", I cried out in jubilation. My daughter looked at me questioningly. "Dad, are you all right?"

El mundo espiritual nueve

"When you see an impurity just blow it out with your intention", Morales told me later. "When dark energy disappears, then only light can take its place", he explained to me.

"Yes, but...", I said.

"No buts, just do it", he ordered.

I sold my companies. I could simply no longer live in this old, traditional world of moneymaking. The process of breaking away from my old life happened swiftly. First it was the Fridays that I reserved for healing sessions. Then came every other Thursday, then every Thursday, then the Wednesdays...

My doubts dispersed. I had great success with the healing, and the clients wrote me mails about it. This feedback encouraged me, because it was the successful healings that made me a name, not marketing.

For the first time in my life, I really had the feeling that I was doing something meaningful. I helped humans and by that time could also make a living from it.

With time, I started getting into esoteric literature a little. Amazing! The things I discovered were unbelievable. I found it extremely interesting just how many people were following this path.

But what was even more interesting were the things that I had learned through the extensive work with clients (at that time I already had nearly 1,000 clients around the world). I had never read books on that subject. It was the practice, the spirits, the feedback of the clients and my reflecting on it that had trained me. In the books I often found confirmation and learned the esoteric terminology.

"Channelling", for example, must be what I was doing while communicating with the spirits, trying to find out what was the matter with the client.

Talking with deceased energies would also come under the term "channelling" or "mediumistic work". Persons who used the assistance of spirits or helpers from the spiritual world during healings were called "mediums". Ok, I thought, then I am a medium too.

Yet these terms were of no importance for me. It was interesting to see how others would try to put into words a subject as difficult to comprehend as energy medicine.

Because actually the issue here was to regain one's own intuition, and to strengthen the seeing ability as well as the proper use of the natural power of intention.

It was all the more interesting to read literature about incredible healing methods, complicated affirmation techniques, complicated exercises. "Healing is a process of consciousness", is a sentence written by a well-known promoter of alternative healing methods, whose books sell very well. "Healing is a process of consciousness"... this is something that one has to sit and think about. And believe me – no one can really understand this sentence. And what does it mean anyway?

As I gained experience it became increasingly clear how simple the way nature had provided for healing was. How simple it was, if one could regain his natural powers to bring about healing.

Define the problem (intuitive feeling), find it (seeing) and simply blow it out (intent): that's all there is to it. Anyone can learn that. Everyone must learn that again, I became more and more aware. To do so, one did not have to travel to Peru or Siberia or Hawaii. To do so it doesn't take a journey into the jungle.

All the more surprised I was when I received a mail from Peru one day. It was very brief, and came from Don Chino, one the young Peruvian shamans. He wrote that I should come to Peru. As soon as possible. The Inca elders wanted to see me.

"The Inca elders want to see me", I said to myself. I didn't need any Incas, I thought at that moment. The knowledge, the healing spirits are just there for everyone to use. Everyone can learn that again and regain the lost knowledge. Besides, I'm not an Indian, I further argued, not wanting to go.

I forgot about the mail for a few days. I didn't need to travel to Peru to gain something from there. I didn't think much of this healing tourism which by then had also reached Germany. Indians were flown in, Peruvians who performed mass healings, healers from Hawaii, Ayuhuasca ceremonies were staged in the south of Germany; it all seemed totally out of place to me. I had many of the participants of such events in my practice for follow-up sessions afterwards, because they couldn't cope with what they had experienced. Nonetheless, I do value the work of these healing importers very highly, as they make people more sensitive and draw attention to this cause. Thank you for that.

"We all have the knowledge. Here. We must only discover it again", the spirits told me during one of my sessions.

Energetic possessions: the war is not yet over

One can quickly recognize possessions in the energy fields of clients, provided one can see energies. We can picture them as someone energetically going along with or hanging on to the client. One can recognise from the clothes, the hair, or the face of these possessions whether they are male or female entities, and how old they are. One can also speak to these energies – because that's what they are – about their psychodramas and ask them where they come from, how they lived and how they died.

75

Most of these possessions are very scared, desperate creatures who haven't managed the transition to light, or did not attempt it for fear.

Many clients know about them, and often even comment about feeling possessed. Inner self-conversations with someone strange, the feeling of not being able to make the decisions ourselves, not to live our life or be able to practice "our" vocation can be signs of a possession.

Verena

Verena is 28 years old and cannot bear to be with men, neither on a personal nor on a professional or any other level, she says. This is the case in all areas of her life, even with things as ordinary as when she gets into a taxi and the driver is a man. This is naturally problematic in the long run, especially now that she has finished her studies and is looking for a permanent job.

Verena was suffering from a very aggressive and anxious male possession, whose energy manifested itself in Verena's life through the total rejection and extreme fear of men.

By explaining this, I am not trying to generate an unnecessary fear of this subject. These possessions are just "energies" – though of a very, very strong kind. We should always keep in mind that they are not beasts which energetically cling onto us, but mostly the energies of the dead in the shape of images, of people who had a great fear of dying and want to live on inside us, hoping to escape death.

Approximately two-thirds of the clients who come to see me are occupied by such energies. These energies have totally different origins. Many of these energies are our grandparents, who experienced the wars. Wars are times of great fears. Fear for survival, fear of dying, the resolution to somehow pull through at any cost, the fight for survival in the trenches. Sixty percent of all the possessions (entities) I encounter are war possessions, energies of people who died in the war.

Seventy percent of my clients with job-related problems come to me because of intimidation and bullying at work – the working environment can be like a battleground. Bullying means betrayal, intrigue, humiliation, exclusion, cheating. I am here, the others are there. As soon as you have or show a weakness, it's your turn. But we know this from somewhere, don't we: most of these clients "carry" possessions from the Second World War. Although the war ended on 8 May 1945, energetically it's not over by a long shot – it just continues on other levels.

I recognize war entities from the clothes and uniforms they "energetically" wear in the energy field of a client: soldier's uniforms, Gestapo overcoats. So they live on energetically and affect the life of other people in all areas to an extreme: in the choice of a partner, at work, with one's hobbies, preferences, clothes, life attitude, courage, fears, nightmares and behaviour in all situations. A client with a possession always behaves like a fusion of himself and someone else.

Peace, real peace in people occurs only when these possessions, these living energies, are released by a shaman and led to the "light" carefully. Then bullying should no longer exist in our world.

El mundo espiritual diez

Five months later at eight in the evening Peruvian time, the bus was waiting for me outside the hotel. I was frightened. Don Chino, one the young shamans who was also the translator of the Inca language Quechua into Spanish, had asked me in the morning to drive to the mountains with the Inca elders and another six shamans. They wanted to hold a special session with me, a mixture of initiation, healing and "Despacho" – whatever that meant.

"Why me of all people?", I asked him several times nervously. "No me preguntes tanto", he kept telling me. "Don't ask so many questions."

So at 20:00 I got on the bus that was full of Q'ero, the descendants of the Incas. Don Humberto, Dona Bernadina, Don Pasqual, Don Chino, Don Francisco, Don Pertí. Only Chino spoke Spanish.

"Chino, quando llagamos?", I asked in a shaky voice. „When will we arrive?"
   "No sé… en una horita o ago asi!". "In one hour", he said. I wanted to ask what they wanted to do with me up there. My head was swimming with images from voodoo films and Mickey Rourke, chickens with their heads chopped off and drinking their blood. These thoughts sent a shiver down my spine. My imagination was running wild: I hope I'm not part of the prophecy, according to which one day a white European – very likely a German – had to be sacrificed to bring salvation to the world… Suddenly my mobile phone beeped: out of range. Isolated. In a bus with six Q'ero. Lost.

Only the picture of my family on the phone's display reminded me of home, and my fear kept asking the question: "Will I ever get back?"

"Stop that now!", I ordered myself. "Look at you; you are shit-scared!". But my apprehension did not abate.

It was dark up there, at an altitude of 4,000 metres. Very dark. We got out of the bus and went into a wooden hut, where a woman made something to eat. For the next two hours, everyone sat around comfortably and ate. And I was in the middle of it, in a blue funk. Everyone spoke in Quechua, and Don Chino was too tired to translate everything to me. I was too tired to ask. Help!

When would they start whatever they wanted to do? It was already eleven at night.

Half an hour later Don Pasqual went away. When he came back he said "listo" – we can begin.

Energy-resonance

At the beginning we already established what the first words of my mentor meant: the way we experience the outside world is a mirror of our inner world. Never in reverse.

Energy disturbances manifest themselves not only on the interior but also on the outside: wretched life circumstances, wrong friends and partner, unsatisfactory job and so on.

An imbalance in one's inner energy has always a one-hundred-percent manifestation on the exterior. People coming to me with an issue such as "lack of self-confidence, deficient thinking", will have trouble making it big in the real world.

Imagine a client who carries two possessions from the war plus other "black stains". This client would probably find it extremely difficult to believe in a world that is safe and without dangers. This person is likely to lead a very safe life, lock his door three times at night, put money aside for a rainy day and be very suspicious of others.

After the sessions, most clients ask what they are supposed to do now. Quit their job? Ask their boss for a raise in salary? End their relationship? Move houses? Emigrate? "Nothing", I tell them always. It is absolutely essential that we don't take any action. For if we are internally cleansed after the treatment, we attract "clean things". When we are "clean", energy spreads. When we are full of energy, our environment changes, and happiness finds us. Then things happen automatically, without any effort on our part. Our circumstances change for the better, our charisma is contagious to others, our enthusiasm and new-found curiosity for life show effect: suddenly we find a partner (he/she comes to us –"coincidence", you might say), everything in the relationship works better than ever before, we attract the people we always wanted to meet, the road to a career is opened, and often one thing follows the other. For in the same way that it attracts the good towards you, it also resonates from you. The smile you send out returns to you. People love you. Love is the highest human form of energy. This is resonance, energetically seen.

Even after thousands of treatment sessions, I am still astonished by the amount of feedback reporting positive changes in the circumstances of my clients. Houses or apartments that had been very difficult to sell were sold almost immediately, new ones have just come to them, a new partner has more or less appeared at the doorstep, the relationship with their children has suddenly improved, orders have been coming in, or an excellent job offer…

You must believe me: mere trying, fighting or overworking is not enough to achieve your goals, because you don't follow the energy flow of the universe. This energy flow will evolve only when we become energetically "pure", when we find the right path. Then everything will find itself automatically. It simply comes to us.

This way of healing is one in which the wounds are transformed into sources of power. The results are evident not only through the healing of the illness, of the symptom, but also, and this often happens very very soon, in the peripheral things in life.

This is basically our greatest chance. Through our healing our quality of life improves. Through our healing new possibilities are created in life. Real alternatives, perspectives, perhaps a new future.

There are no coincidences in life. In the Envisioning course the pupils learn to read the signs (coincidences) of the future. The word coincidence comes from coincide, derived from the Latin co-incidere, which means"to fall upon". As we can see, originally this word had a completely different meaning, and so it becomes clear that we are not victims of coincidences, but that things or situations fall upon us, that they are products of our progress through life. Consequently, what falls upon us is only that with which we are in resonance.

A simple example of resonance is that we, one way or another, always meet people who are compatible with us. Whenever I give seminars, the participants always form small individual groups immediately. There might be one group of people who come from the same area, another group that perhaps already has some shamanic knowledge from before, or yet another consisting of people who have already attended several courses of this kind. It could be groups of businesspeople, physicians, nurses, yoga teachers. The participants come from all walks of life, most of them have no prior knowledge, some are from Austria, others from Switzerland, but all are interested in the topic "working energetically". People in such groups have things in common, they feel relaxed, and it is easy to get to know each other.

Later, when they get to know each other better, the groups reform completely. Then the weary ones come together, the merry ones, the smokers, people sharing the same world views. Exactly this is the level of energy, the level of resonance. We could bend over backwards, but we would still attract those people who we like "energetically".

"Tell me who you go out with and I will tell you who you are", says the proverb. If we have a high degree of energetic pollution, then we attract others who live in the same condition. Anything else is not possible, since we want to spend time with someone who understands us. An optimist will not bear a lethargic depressive for a long time. This is also why the rich always become richer, and the poor poorer. But if we can heal ourselves we can break through this resonance cycle.

Carmen

Energetic possessions and their resonance can even send us to foreign countries, as the example of Carmen shows. Carmen is from Colombia but lives in Barcelona. She no longer knows what she's supposed to do in Europe. She's been living in Spain for ten years, is alone again, but can't go back to Colombia. She is "caught in a trap", she says. She learned Italian in Milan, now she is back in Barcelona, but she can't really settle anywhere. All this makes her very sad, especially when she looks into the future and asks herself what she's suppose to do with her life… then she begins to cry. "I don't know why I cry", she says. "I never wanted to live it up, but now my business is doing badly, I feel alone, and I just don't know where to go."

I start with the treatment quickly, because I don't want her to relive her drama. In her third chakra I see her as a maid in a previous life. She is standing in a bedroom making the beds, when a man comes in and begins to hit her. He speaks French and says something like: "You are just a servant, you are not to interfere in our affairs."

"But I haven't!", she says.

"Then from whom has my wife found out about us? You must have spoken about it with the others, you can't keep your mouth shut." Enraged, the man grabs her by the throat and strangles her.

The follow-up conversation with Carmen reveals a lot: "Yes", she says, "the image is interesting. I've always had poorly paid jobs. I've always been scared to take on responsibility, because I thought that I would be punished for what I do. There's also an association with French. When I was young, I always had the feeling that I had to go to France. I've also lived there for three years. Hadn't I told you that? I've always had the feeling that there was still something to be done there."

I was happy to appease her: not only was the aggressive male energy led to the light during the session, but her entire trauma was energetically eliminated.

Four months later we received a mail from Carmen. She was back home in Colombia and was very happy to have ended a journey that had taken nearly ten years.

El mundo espiritual once

"Listo" —"we can begin", said Pasqual. "Begin with what?", I asked myself, swallowing the last potato. This is what we had for dinner. Together with meat, chicken, I think. It was burned and tasted of charcoal.

Everyone rose, went outside, into another wooden hut and sat down on the ground. It was cold, I could see the stars, and the mountains looked like the teeth of an ogre. Small crucifixes were scattered around the hut, ceremonial artefacts, candles. It smelled of sage. It was pitch-black. The candles gave off some light and the flickering produced funny creatures and shadows on the faces of the Incas. I was very very scared, and alone.

They began to build a small altar with coca leaves, a kind of offering for the spirits. This is offered to the light during a fire ceremony, I remembered having read somewhere. They passed the coca leaves around to everyone. Everyone blew an intention, a wish, into the leaves and returned them to the elder, who then added them to the altar again.

What wish should I blow into the leaf, I thought. "I want to get out of here healthy", I blew as my first wish and gave the coca leaf to Don Humberto. He thanked me, blew something into it too and put it back on the altar.

"If I get out of here, then I would like to be happy with what I do", was my next wish. The other Q'ero did the same. I was curious as to what wishes they had blown into the coca leaves.

"What is going on?", I thought. "Why have they chosen me?"

The ceremony went on for at least two hours, and I became more and more anxious. Anxiety, I thought, is always an omen of what comes next. If I could look behind the scenes, I would probably be surprised how much had already happened in the last two hours.

"Listo", said Don Humberto and blew out the candles. I had never in my life seen such darkness before. Suddenly I felt a hand on my back, and another on my stomach. I was to lie down – which I did. My heart was beating like mad, and I was sweating. Other hands took my shoes off and held my feet. Hopefully they're not sweaty, I thought. My fear had reached a climax. I shuddered when someone put his warm hands on my temples.

I heard the other Q'ero whisper in Quechua. Were they talking about me? I had no control of the situation at all. If someone pulled a knife now they could kill me without a sound. I am at their mercy, I thought. Is this perhaps my issue which should be healed? Trust? Will I be healed at all? I heard whistles, smelled spices. And this incessant whispering. Then I heard someone whistle… like my father always used to whistle on weekends when he was off work. Someone blew over my body, then again. It was as if someone blew a coat of chains off me. Then I saw the face of an Indian. "What's your name?", I asked. "Don Mariano". "Don Mariano?" I don't know a Don Mariano. Don Mariano disappeared from my fantasy, and then I saw a green meadow with flowers… in the summer.

All of a sudden it was bright, very bright. It was as if someone was holding a flashlight to my face. The hands on my face indicated that I should open my eyes. The candles seemed to have come on again. How was that possible?

"Listo", said Don Humberto. "Finished." "Yes, but… ", I thought and asked Chino, who spoke Spanish: "Chino, I feel lighter and freer, but what happened exactly? What was this thing with the altar?" "Vas a ver", said Chino. "You will see."

They went outside all together. I don't know how, but there was a fire, a big fire, already burning 50 metres away. The Q'ero went there with the altar, which actually is called Despacho, Chino told me. They would take the Despacho, all my wishes, my healing, "to the light" – offer it to the fire. I was not allowed to be there, said Chino. If I watched, the Despacho would not go to the light. I should go back to the hut and rest – maybe sleep a little.

I couldn't sleep, of course. I sat in the hut with my ears pricked. I could hear the Q'ero singing a ceremonial song and wasn't sure what was happening to me – or rather to my

Despacho. After about an hour the singing stopped – they seemed to be finished.

"I have to know what happened to me and why they did all this just for me" I decided, and caught Chino before he went to sleep.

„Chino!", I called. „Martin", he replied. „Chino …para qué todo eso?"„What was all this for?", I asked him.

"Acuestate", said Chino."Go to bed", fending me off.

„Chino..quiero saber porque!" I want to know why! Please tell me!

Chino looked at me. He was tired and annoyed by my questioning. He hesitated, turned, checked whether his elder master Don Humberto was watching him, and said curtly:

"Martin: vas a ser curandero con mucho éxito"."Martin, you will become a great shaman". And with these words he left me alone.

TREATMENT, DESTINY AND HAPPINESS

The treatment

Martin, you must describe in more detail what you see, and most importantly it must become clearer what is so extraordinary about this 'spiritual medicine', as you call it", says my co-author.

It is Thursday again – my writing day.

"It's not easy to write about it; I mean, the fantastic thing about this medicine is its simplicity."

"Then describe this simplicity."

"You can talk. It is the complicated things one can write pages about."

"Martin, just write how simple this medicine is. What happens during a treatment? Just describe an energetic session – it will help to clarify things!", he says.

"The treatment is very simple. The client comes with an issue, mental, physical or a mixture of both. We talk about it for two or three minutes, and by then I can already see the energy disturbance that causes it. The client selects a stone from a variety of stones that I present to him. This stone must be picked instinctively to correspond to his problem the closest. Then the client blows his problem into the stone, puts it on the treatment table, and I begin to work with him. As soon as I see the disturbance, I can just remove it, like a weed. And because the source of the illness is energetically eliminated, the problem disappears too."

"How do you take out the energy disturbance? With a stone?"

"No, the stone is a kind of energy storage device; it stores the issue of the client and informs me. Stones are very wise; they are millions of years old and support the healer in his work. The stone is then placed on the chakra of the client that is affected. In this way the dark energy from this chakra can be transferred into the stone. In addition, I see the energy disturbance and can blow it out with my breath and with my intent. I never touch the client."

"You mean there's no diagnosis, no lengthy preliminary discussions about the problems, no medications? You just blow it out?". He is surprised.

"That's how simple it is if one can see energies and learns how to extract energy disturbances from the luminous energy field of the client with one's own intent."

"So this means that people come to you, tell you their problem (just for a couple of minutes), then you blow out the problem or illness, and it disappears?"

What definitely disappears is the energy disturbance which has become visible through the verbalisation of the problem or illness. Of course, one cannot predict how long it takes for the illness to disappear. Physical problems might need some time to heal, as the body is at the end of the healing chain of "energy, soul, mind, body".

As a spiritual healer or shaman, I may not make promises, but the healing chances of this medicine are very substantial.

The shamanic way of healing is one of power. It is a way of nature. For it is not the healer who heals the client, but ultimately the client who heals himself. All the healer does is to activate one's self-healing powers.

El mundo espiritual doce

"Martin, you will become a great healer...". Back to my practice in Cologne, this sentence was still ringing in my ears. How does one become a great healer, I asked myself. And what does that mean anyway: "You will become a great healer"?

"Fantastic...", I whispered to myself. Pictures of great healers such as Joau de Deus crossed my mind. I saw myself on a large stage in front of thousands of people who were all healed by me. This image made me laugh. These are superstar visions, I thought.

The desires of a teenager who finally wants to become big. Is this what Chino meant?

The long-distance treatment

Lars

Lars's wife accuses him of always "shutting down" and becoming unapproachable when she talks to him. He, on the other hand, is always afraid of being inadequate – of not delivering what others expect from him, and that torments him, he says.

We hang up. Long-distance treatment basically works just as person-to-person treatment. First we briefly speak about the issue – the client blows the problem into the telephone receiver while I hold one of the healing stones by the receiver, so that the stone takes in the energy of the client. Then we put the phone down and start to work.

I hold the stone in my hand and feel Lars's energy, which is now stored in it as information, like a copy. I close my eyes and with my intent I transform myself and Lars's energy field into the "treatment room" of the spirits, where we begin to work. Any change in Lars's energy field that occurs in the treatment room is then passed to him. Lars will tell me about it later.

I look at Lars's energy field – it seems totally black in the centre, like a volcano. Near the third chakra, where the solar plexus is, I see two pipes, connections to the outside. They look like umbilical cords. They lead to two feminine energies, to two living women. A shaman can at some point feel whether an energy is male or female. I go along one of the cords to this energy, and I see the image of a very dominant but affectionate woman, the all-protective mother type. The other connection goes to a younger woman, also dominant, strict. I separate the connection and observe how the chakra spins in fresh light. It already looks much brighter.

Then I wait for two or three minutes for the energy field to regain its balance and I go into his third chakra again – this time a little bit deeper. It is dark in there, very dark. I clean it, and now I can see a platform in the fog. It is enormous, maybe 30 meters tall. Lars is standing on it. I see hands. Hands surrounding the platform. I continue from the hands over the arms, remove dark energies, and see the face of an old woman. She is distraught; she wants to die, is filled with bitterness, perhaps even anger. She is very much afraid of dying.

I remove the platform, eliminate the dark energy and see how one of the severed connections wants to "come back". Now I remove all the dark, foggy residual energies in this chakra. The connection disappears again.

I speak to the old woman, ask her whether she doesn't want to finally come to the "light" after all the years. She is frightened. She insults me, screams at me to go away. I offer her a better future than in Lars's body, a future in light and love. She thinks, hesitates and finally consents. I lead her to the light and see two spirits coming to assist. They gently take her and pull her up and through a light channel. Now the chakra transforms itself into a wonderful, spinning disk of caring light.

I look at the clock. The treatment has taken twenty minutes.

Lars calls and tells me what he experienced. He tells me of a deep gloominess that had suddenly disappeared, and of pictures of old people and landscapes he saw that he didn't know. His body feels warm, he says. He could say that much already. He also feels calmer, he says.

"Well, let's wait for a while", I tell the clients often, because the deep energetic changes will look for manifestation on the exterior. This will certainly happen. His dominant wife and dominant mother were a result of the inner possession Lars carried within himself, not the other way round. The law of resonance applies always.

After the extraction of this and the other energies Lars's life will change to an extreme extent. Perhaps the relationship with his wife will improve greatly, become more affectionate, and perhaps they will discover each other's new, nice sides. It is however also possible that they will separate. Because the affinity, the control issue in Lars's energy field has been eliminated – it no longer exists.

If the healing benefits from a separation, then it is totally normal and a step in the right direction.

El mundo espiritual trece

The questions after the consultations were always the same: "Martin, how can it be that I feel better? I mean, I blow my issue into one of these stones, you rattle it a bit, then blow and my sleep disorder is gone. It can't possibly be so simple – how does it work? How do you do it?". That was a standard question after every treatment session.

At first, when I had only 2-3 sessions a day, I was able to answer these questions in depth and tell the clients quite a lot about healing mythology, energy, light and such, but when the number of daily sessions increased this was no longer possible. I had to cut the "after-treatment" short – I couldn't offer much background information. So at first I started recommending books, then films, and then someone suggested that I hold a brief seminar, at which I could talk to those interested about various energy techniques. That was a good idea.

The seminars always consist of two parts: the first part is informative; it describes energy medicine, how healing works, why we often feel unwell, why we are or become ill and what the causes for the symptoms are. It is about energy, about the fact that we are all connected, and about how easy it is to be healed.

During the second part of the seminar I always perform a healing journey with all participants. In his fantasy, the participant travels back to the time when the origin of his illness manifested itself and heals his trauma in the past, thus healing at the same time his problems in the Here and Now.

I always describe this group healing journey as "casual". A proper healing journey that is normally accomplished during an individual treatment, not in a group, is a far more in-depth experience. This "soul retrieval" can heal the most serious illnesses.

It was on a Saturday in April – by then I had done numerous seminars. The participants were lying on the ground. They had prepared themselves for the journey, had innerly articulated their "issue" (the illness, the symptom, the problem, psychological or physical), and were ready to be"led" by me. One of my students was assisting me and accompanied the journey with rhythmic rattles. After ten minutes I closed my eyes and couldn't believe what I saw…

On to happiness

The immensely important clearing of our luminous body is a deeply energetic process.

One can compare the energy balance of a normal human being with a dark river full of large dark sacks. These are our heaviest issues.

At the beginning I work with each client three times at the most. The client must prepare himself for the three most difficult issues in his life (diseases, problems, physical or psychological). We begin with the most difficult problem, which often affects the other issues too.

Returning to the above parallel, we basically clear away the heaviest stones from the river, until the river from very dark gradually turns murky and then becomes clearer and clearer.

This work cannot be compared to other styles of therapy, as the treatment here is deeply energetic.

The more of these energetic issues – the black stains in our luminous energy field – we rid ourselves of, the closer we get to our destiny, to happiness in all areas of our life. Because energetic healing transforms our own wounds into sources of power, releases us from old burdens, from which we could not emancipate ourselves otherwise.

The South American peoples teach us to shed our past, just like the snake sheds its skin. The deep sense of this picture is the speed it comes to pass. The snake only needs a few days to get rid of its skin – maybe even less.

I experience the healing process of the clients just as fast. People with deep-seated fears, nightmares, gnawing doubts, problems of the most diverse kinds lose these issues in the shortest of times. This goes totally against our western understanding of how long we need to shake off an illness. In our western world everything is associated with achievement, and accordingly we accustom ourselves to a long convalescence. Lengthy therapies are not at all a part of the indigenous cultures. The problem is located and simply removed from the energy field, just blown or taken out. That's it.

Just think of the term"skive off work" that we widely use in our society – no one among the indigenous peoples would "invent" an illness or use an illness as an excuse in order not to have to go to work.

Working with children

It makes no difference whether a shaman works with a child or with an adult, because the shaman always works with the luminous body – and that has no age.

In the institute we also focus on the work with children. A successful removal of an energetic blockade can to a great extent set the course for the life of a child. Working with children is fantastic; children are still able to freely describe their experiences in the shape of pictures. Hyperactivity, neurodermatitis, nervousness, problems at school, separation of the parents, pressure to achieve – these are some of the issues children come to us with, to name but a few.

The importance of a shamanic treatment at an early age is immense: it greatly shapes the future of the child. Imagine the life of a child with a fearful possession in his energy system. In real life, this child will permanently feel pressure and fear – at school, at the kindergarten, anywhere. The child will then develop avoidance strategies to block this fear. For instance, it may be that the child never learns to swim or ride a bicycle or does badly at school because he is frightened. The consequences can be devastating. Therefore it is never too early to start with energetic healing as soon as disturbances arise.

Of course, it is not always possessions that are to blame for such problems. Often it is also energies within the family that settle in the luminous energy field of the child. When parents enquire with us for an appointment to see their children, we usually ask them to come for a consultation first. The reason is that, in every case, children reflect the dramas of their parents. We often see that when a member is healed, the whole family is healed too.

Destiny means therefore to experience happiness in ALL areas of life, to find our life contract, our calling. When we are innerly pure we live in richness, not in want. When we are innerly pure we can only attract pure on the exterior. Then we are ready to attain what we dream of.

Shedding our past like a snake sheds its skin sounds very enticing. Believe me, it is as simple. And with this I go back to my scanty preface. Because we have no more time for illness.

Isn't it a pity when one wrestles with a permanent condition for decades, tormented by the same problem, possessed by the same recurring demon – isn't it a pity when this prevents one from working on the fulfilment of one's actual dreams, one's life contract, one's happiness. We have no time. We must hurry!

A life lasts several decades. An energetic treatment takes about 30 minutes and requires no interdependence, no subsequent work and no mental or financial "reckoning". Because what is gone is gone. Again, for the last time: I never would have thought it possible myself, but I have really experienced it.

You should live your life your whole life long. In perfect happiness. In your life contract. This is the reason you are in this world, why nature created you. You alone by the degree of your healing can allow happiness to become the architect of your life, changing and organising it positively. Because only when you become really healthy can you also attract healthy, bright, and rich things. Your happiness will find you automatically; you will no longer miss the signs.

Nature is generous. Deficiency is not at all one of its objectives – only growth. You are light, love, life. This is my mission, this is the purpose of this book. That's why today is actually the first day of the rest of your life.

Believe me, you will set out on the most exciting journey you've ever experienced. And the most exciting thing about this journey is you! Do not waste time.

El mundo espiritual catorce

In the room that I saw with my eyes closed there were no walls, no doors, no floor. Only energy. I counted the number of rays of light coming from the bodies of the participants: "One, two... eleven, 49... wow!"

I opened my eyes wanting to check whether the luminous bodies were really corresponding to the physical bodies. And they were.

Sweat was running down my back. Even for me, this discovery was eerie. Still, I couldn't stop myself from closing my eyes again. And there it was again: the luminous bodies of the participants, the rays of light up toward to the sky.

But there was more: around the luminous bodies seemed to move creatures of light, and they appeared to be performing an "operation" with a female participant. It seemed that they were "extracting" dark energy from her chakras.

I opened my eyes and thought: "Martin, this time you are really going mad!". I closed my eyes again, and suddenly the whole room was full of healing creatures, full of spirits helping the participants to heal their issues. I counted over 120 spirits, so to speak doctors from the light world who were supporting me during the group journey.

That was when I found out that I could perform mass healings and work as a healing medium. I had reached a new level in my vocation as a healer.

This is why the seminars are now called "mediumistic healing journeys". After this experience I understood a little more what Don Chino had meant when he said goodbye to me back in Peru.

When happiness comes to us: vision

"We are more afraid of the light than of our darkness", someone said once. As I have mentioned here before, most of us are objectors of happiness and destiny.

When we have the most severe wounds in our life healed, our life on the exterior usually changes in the extreme. Those friends who never were real ones leave, new friends take their place, our debts become fewer, we are offered a new job, a new partner finds us, a new place to live too. Unbelievable things can happen, can come into the river if we get rid of our burdens, our fears, our anxieties, our black stains.

Then happiness will come knocking on our door, and it is then that most of us will encounter our most important issue, our largest black stain: the fear of accepting happiness. The fear of saying yes to the changes it will bring along. Of saying yes to the journey on which we must set out.

For no matter how bad things were in the past, we have grown accustomed to it all: to the strategies developed to avoid fear, to the discussions about "how terrible everything is" with our friends, to the "wrestling" for attention because surely we are the worst off. We have got used to smoking stinking cigarettes, knowing full well that smoking is harmful and smokers are often regarded as idiots. We have got used to the neighbourhood we live in, with its dark faces or the petit bourgeois neighbours, to the daily telephone calls from mother who can't let go, to the domineering boss, to the boring partner, even to the bad weather. And for some, healing also has financial consequences: it could be that, after the healing, one will be able to work again – just imagine that!

Many clients come to us with this last issue: the fear of finally jumping into the fresh raging water of life. Because this is just another issue and can also be treated energetically. And when this fear disappears we automatically open the door to let in the fresh fragrance of the summer wind, which will take us in its arms and carry us into a future in paradise, a future full of happiness.

Life contract. Destiny. Happiness.

As I mentioned above we all come into the world with an energetic life contract which needs to be fulfilled – this is the reason for our quest in life. What stops us from "realising" this contract are our energetic disturbances, our black stains.

When most of these stains are erased, this contract will become more active. It will present itself on the exterior, manifest itself. Then we will recognize, we will feel our destiny, because the search will suddenly end, for our life will feel "right". "Right" in the sense of loving, whole, fulsome. What does this mean exactly? How can the energetic life contract present itself in real life?

Earlier in the book we did the exercise of imagining how our life in all its areas (job, partnership, mental health, physical health) would be, if there were no "yes, but"s. The readers who did that short hypothetic exercise will have realised that the vision was heavenly.

And this is exactly what our life contract contains purely "energetically": a life in paradise, a life in richness. More is not possible.

Which specific job will come up along our way, how our future partner will be, how much weight we will lose or gain, how stable we will be psychologically – all of this remains to be seen. But one thing is certain, and this we can trust: nature and the universe will support us with all their powers.

Some clients experience the change in their life in a very dramatic manner and in a very rapid process. During the transition from our past mediocre life to a healed life, the dark house which we lived in can collapse very quickly. This transitional phase can be painful, as many of our old patterns will disappear. This can become evident physically and mentally, but also on the exterior. Some people who are in the phase of reorganizing their lives –and remember: everything happens automatically, we don't have to do anything actively – complain of an initial deterioration, which, however, is completely normal.

It may sound crazy, but when new clients come to us we always ask them whether they really are prepared to enter the adventure "new life".

Who are our clients?

The people who come to us are those who have the courage to confront their issues. Despite the common belief that the shaman is the last resort ("Well, if nothing else helps, I'll try it"), only few come to us with acute physical illnesses. Such people are advised to seek medical assistance anyway, as energetic treatment cannot substitute the casualty ward of a hospital (it is something that's effective in the long term) or offer quick relief from physical problems.

People from all walks of life come to us with all kinds of issues: the departmental manager who has problems with his staff. The nurse who always rubs her boss the wrong way. The actress who doesn't know why she is always sad. The woman who still suffers from her dominant mother. The businessman who can't let go of his business. The salesperson who can't close any deals, the car dealer who doesn't sell his cars, the life counsellor whose practice is always empty, people who always meet the same type of partner, or just people who are afraid of life.

Among our clients are also people who are compulsively materialistic, possessed by consumerism, and have the associated fear of loss which is very widespread in our consumer and credit-oriented society, adults with sleep disorders and children with all possible symptoms.

Disconnected from ourselves and from everything else

Most people live disconnected from themselves and from everything else. We often receive enquiries from people who just wish to get rid of their "illness" and come to us by recommendation. "We are not physicians, we don't treat illnesses", we have to tell them in such cases. We work on the energetic level and cannot, and may not, promise anything. Yet if your energetic disturbances are removed your life's other aspects will also change; this is the way it works.

Only few are aware of the connection between inner energy, soul, mind, body and external environment. If one works on his inner energy, this automatically has consequences on all areas of life. Most separate the body from the soul ("everything has a psychological origin") and do not make the connection between their exterior life and inner healing.

There are so many human beings who do want to heal their issue but are afraid of letting go, afraid of what will happen then. And it is exactly this fear, the distrust of our inherent direction, that makes us ill. The fear of trusting life and therefore ourselves. If this fear is healed you will land in the warm lap of Mother Earth again, and she will guide you safely.

Happily unhappy

The average reader, including you, will probably realise when reading this book that he is actually not so ill after all. Everything is sort of all right, you will say. And perhaps you are right too. But believe me, my experience says that this "sort of all right" is the most deceitful feeling one can have. This is exactly the standard in quality of life at which we somehow learn to live with everything, even accept that the way we live is okay. But is it really?

During my seminars I ask the participants whether they can identify themselves with the following statements:

"My job isn't bad, it brings money in and it's safe... of course I'd rather write books or make a living from my art, music, riding my bicycle, fishing, or whatever else, but..."

"My relationship is okay. Of course, one can't have everything, but…"

"I actually feel reasonably healthy, except that from time to time I suffer from backache, I am nervous, stressed, or feel rushed, but this is normal nowadays …"

Most people to whom these answers apply trundle through life; sometimes there are "highs", maybe through a new love, or a motivational shove with a new job, but when the novelty wears off their life trundles along again. No improvement, a permanent discontentment and the annoying issue of the search for something that will finally make them happy.

So if you identify yourselves a little in these examples, you have already found a fund of issues that can be energetically worked on.

What comes afterwards?

Then comes the creation. Once in this state, we have achieved a high inner purity. The struggle and the search are almost over, and we discover two amazing things: we are creators of our own life, and we are aided by tremendous powers.

There are an incredible number of books in relevant literature that have been written on this subject too: about the notion that we can resolve to be happy, empowerment books like "The power is within us" etc. They are all right.
I don't know how you felt after reading these books; I always felt very enthusiastic while reading them, because everything was so clear and logical. I mainly read before going to bed,

so I would fall asleep content and with my head full of great new inspirations. But when I woke up everything had disappeared, all the wise words and sentences.

Everyday life – real life – is different. The more of these "life counsellor books" I read, the more impotent and helpless I felt. Try and tell a depressive person with possessions inside him that he is the creator of his life. The only thing you will achieve is to give him feelings of guilt.

For the "inner" clearing, the energetic extraction of one's burdens as a tool, a method, for getting rid of one's problems properly and for a long time, was not mentioned anywhere.

I had the immense fortune to regain old energetic knowledge; better said, it returned to me.

This knowledge lies dormant in each one of us. Just as happiness in life waits for us.

My destiny is to spread this knowledge and, by doing so, to bring people onto the path of happiness. How do I know that? Because I do it with extreme joy and devotion.

Let your happiness, your destiny, come to you. Those who do it with their whole heart will be aided in the realization by amazing powers. Then your visions, if they come from the heart, will have real power.

You could now put this booklet aside; tomorrow you will be confronted by your everyday life. But now there is a difference: you now know that a chance exists, that there is a possibility to transform your traumas into sources of power.

Happiness will then come to you automatically. You just need the courage to do it.

El mundo espiritual quince

By now there was not a single evening in which I didn't contact the spirits. I would travel along the ray of light, past the stars and the moon, the spirit would open the door for me and I would enter the magnificent room, decorated with precious stones.

They explained to me the entrusting of the seeing rights, and that I was one of few qualified to show and teach others how to "see" energies.

The link of the third eye to the heart chakra has been described in many books. The spirits however taught me how to install it in the luminous energy field of the client, so that the student could learn to see very quickly. They taught me how to open the third eye of the participants.

Within the following weeks I set up my Energy School. The first course (Foundation course) was booked out just two weeks after its publication on the Internet.

Those who follow the way of the heart, who put their heart into what they do, will be aided by the whole universe. For the assistance of the spirits is infinite. "You call the spirit, and the spirit answers" – always.

I was so delighted with my abilities that I took off in a flight of fancy. I had a unique gift in me, and I kept reaching new heights of healing every time. In the beginning there was the success in the sessions, then the work with the spirits during the sessions, then the group healings... I was over the moon, and I decided to have a ceremony one day as a way of showing my gratitude.

The spirits' reply was: "Thank you, but don't be so full of self-importance always; you must have a consultation about it with one of your students."

'This is getting better and better here...'. I was shocked. The spirits challenged me all the time. I should have myself treated by my students? Because I take myself too seriously?

Okay. I didn't argue. I just did it. During one course I asked a student whether she would like to work with me. She was flabbergasted, but consented. "This is not on", came from my ego. "You can't lower yourself to the level of the student".

The spirit interfered: "There are three reasons for doing it. First: it is time to lose your ego. Second: it is time to give up all the separation in your life. There is no teacher. There are no students. We all learn from one another. Third: the only way to make the school really big is that you train the best healers. Prove it by having one of them treat you."

I hesitated for a long time before I did it. But afterwards I was free. I no longer had an ego. I had left my ego trip behind. Every graduate of the Energy School is a very good healer. Thank you, spirit. Hatun Chasca.

The end

Testimonials

These testimonials were written both by participants of the Energy School and by our clients. In order to preserve authenticity, the texts are unabridged and not revised linguistically (except for being translated from German). The following reports are only a small selection of the testimonials that reach us.

•

Hello Martin,

I know the institute is closed this week, but I must tell you this now.

What you told us was not new to me. Wicca for example has many parallels, connections that exist etc.

You probably know this too.

I felt though that Sunday summed it all up at last. It was wonderful.

During the introduction I had said that I was looking and now I am a little bit on the way and feel very well.

If I hadn't already enrolled for the Foundation Course in January, I would have done it on Saturday at the latest.

I did not go on the healing journey thinking of pain, but with the search for direction and answers in mind. The security I feel now is a little bit scary, but I want to venture it. Luckily the pain on my shoulder has almost disappeared and I'm happy about it.

I'm really looking forward to the Foundation course and am very excited about it.

Did you know that I would write this?

Sincerely kind regards and a little sunshine from
Angelika

•

Dear Martin,

Today, two days after the healing journey my pain is nearly gone and the huge wounds that had remained after the infection have stopped suppurating and are as good as healed overnight. Of course it will take a while before they disappear and they will leave big scars, but that doesn't bother me. At last no more sleeping tablets! Although I have learned in the meantime from the bittersweet nightwork to transform the severe pain into heat, this hasn't always been possible because I couldn't summon up the concentration. Somehow we've both had the feeling that once we get over this illness something new would begin, something that has got to do with our common life's work and that a lot of things, including ourselves, will change.

We are eagerly expecting it....

We thank Mother Earth for her wisdom, for arranging that we met you, and we thank you for your love.

Even though we know you have very little time, we would greatly appreciate a reply from you, Martin.

Love from Udo too,
Johanna

•

Hello Martin,

I read your little book. You could have been a short story writer: pleasant, direct and ironic at the same time.

I like that, because most people in the esoteric and healing circles tend to be up in the clouds.

Enough praise. The reason I'm writing to you is because I am hoping to learn something from you…

Chris

•

Hello dear Martin,

This is the not totally hopeless yet very difficult case writing.

Your words are still ringing in my ears.

I have the feeling you would perhaps be pleased about some feedback. My last healing journey with you did me a lot of good. After the first session, unfortunately for me quite negative effects became apparent. But I hope that the worst is now behind me. In addition I am making an effort to comply with the request of the spirits and "sit still". And yet I would like to continue, as soon as possible, because for a long time now I've had the feeling that I'm leading a completely wrong life. Your last healing journey brought me so many indescribably valuable gifts, and for that I would like to thank you again. Thank you!!!

My friends liked it too, there's only one little thing that they brought up a few times, namely that they had the feeling they were "rushed" from one room to the next during the journey. It all went much too quickly, so it was difficult to be aware of and pick up everything. This is no criticism, only an account of what they told me.

I hope you're feeling as fine as I do at the moment. Thank you!!!

Maybe I'll call you on Monday to find out when I can carry on, and what the next step is. Until Monday!!! Have a nice weekend, P.

•

Good morning Martin,

Thank you for your mail. The treatment did me good. I feel a lot better. I still feel a light "rumbling" in my stomach. Maybe I need another treatment. At the moment I feel a lot more relaxed and calmer.

Love Ute

•

Hello Herr Brune,

My scepticism has now left me. I haven't had any pain in my leg for eight weeks now. At first I thought it was only a phase, but the pain hasn't returned at all. The only thing is that I always think about it. But it doesn't hurt anymore. I shouldn't be thinking about it so much, I know... so I'll stop and relish it!!!

Many many thanks,
H.R.

•

In spring 2005 we had a very heavy storm. I was at the sports studio at the time. When I went back to my car I was shocked to find two thick tree branches lying next to it. The car was covered with soil, tree bark and branches. The roof had several dents and scratches. The windshield was completely smashed. The strange thing though was that all the other cars on the parking lot were completely unharmed, only mine was hit!

This incident gave me cause for thought, and I had the feeling that it may have been a sign. I tried to work it out: Car roof with dents, car has to do with autonomy. Is something hitting against my autonomy or am I too much of a head person (roof)? How can I see clearer again (windshield)? I spoke with a friend and colleague of mine, and he said I should separate myself from something old (symbolically "old branches").

My car insurance paid me 1,500 euros compensation for the storm damage.

In May 2005 I met Martin Brune through a friend. I first went to him as a client. I experienced my first healing treatment, and was moved, deeply impressed and relieved. Since the treatment I've had, and still have, the feeling as if a heavy load has been taken from me. Since then I feel lighter, freer and more connected. The old things (see old branches) were old energies, old connections, which were eliminated through the healing.

I decided to attend Martin's foundation seminar. I had already received the 1,500 euros from my car insurance. Afterwards I attended the Energy School and now work with Martin Brune as an assistant by the hour in the practice of the Shamanic Healing Institute. I see the work there as a valuable addition for me personally, and also for my work as a teacher of children with special needs, child therapist and alternative practitioner. The quickly-achieved healing successes that I frequently experience never cease to impress me still today.

Following some case examples:

One of my first clients was my mother; she had been taking 1-2 laxative tablets every day for 20 years. During the first treatment things started to work in my mother's intestines, and we could hear loud noises from her stomach and bowels. My mother had three bowel movements on the same day and hasn't needed laxatives ever since.

Some weeks ago I treated in the practice a young client who came for a second treatment. Upon my question how she had been doing after the first treatment with Martin, she told me that her sleep disorder and nightmares, from which she had

113

suffered for over 20 years, had disappeared. She had been receiving medical treatment and psychotherapy for years.

Another young client came to me for a third healing treatment. Martin was unexpectedly unable to see her on that day. When I told her that she said it was perfectly alright if I treated her; she trusted my abilities. In her previous – second – treatment which she'd had with me alone, her issue was her increased testosterone level and her disturbed menstruation cycle, which she'd had for years. She'd had no more bleeding for over a year. She'd underwent hormone treatment for years but to no avail. Five days after her second shamanic healing session her period started again.

My sister experienced relief from her cold feet after treatment. A friend reported that after the treatment she feels more together, senses herself more and strains herself less innerly with the problems of others. Another friend was able to process more easily the unexpected death of her mother. I distance-treated her. The remarkable thing with her was that I had used a healing joss stick from the Himalayas. After the long-distance treatment my friend said that she had smelled the scent of a joss stick from Asia, and that she felt safer and more secure than before. I could name and describe many similar examples, but it would be out of proportion in this context. Love, Elke

•

Hello Martin,

Thank you for the wonderful session yesterday – I feel sooo much better than on the day before, reinvigorated and no longer so gloomy and sad. I look forward to the follow-up, S.F.

•

Hello Martin,

After our session I've been feeling liberated, and the fear hasn't appeared since. I was very impressed about how accurately you saw the images of my inner world.

Many thanks and kind regards from Berlin,

C.

•

Christina Secker

Graphic designer / budding singer / soon-to-be life coach from Munich

I had three shamanic healing sessions with Herr Brune. However I will describe only the first session here in greater detail, as this is the most interesting to be described. I would not like to have missed any of these sessions, even though the second one was not as successful as the first and the third, partly also due to my still existing over-intellectualised approach. I would like to seize the opportunity of giving my view on shamanic work in this book to emphasise that such work must become a standard in our current health system!

I would like to encourage all people, because health and healing are possible! But only if we give the shamans, alternative practitioners and homoeopaths, among others, a chance to heal us in natural ways and stop blindly trusting all-brain physicians who, by prescribing all these pharmaceutical medicines for many years, have brought us more illness than we can imagine.

In the first session with Herr Brune we dealt with my issue of "vocation".

Due to my many talents I often feel tugged this way and that as regards career, so I wanted to have more clarity for myself. In addition I wanted to lose the inner pressure that has been building up from that. I wanted to feel joy and have fun with everything I do or at least to stop reproaching myself, stop listening to the negative babbling of my ego (thoughts): "You must still take care of this" or "You haven't done that yet" etc. I definitely wanted to get rid of that.

After Herr Brune and I had located the issue in about four minutes, I breathed with my existing emotion three times into the telephone receiver and put the telephone down. I relaxed on my futon, closed my eyes and waited to see what would happen. After about five minutes I felt like something, it could have been a staff, was moving in my heart chakra in circles. That was all that I was able to perceive from the first session. Unfortunately I did not sense images or any other emotions, but the rotary movement in my heart chakra impressed me very much.

After the session I called Herr Brune again and we discussed what he had found. Herr Brune explained to me that, among other things, the vision of life is located in the heart chakra. There he detected a male energy caught in a kind of bear trap, which was holding me captive, so to speak. With a huge effort, he was able to open this trap, and the male energy left me and flew upward in the shape of a ray of light.

After the treatment I didn't feel anything in particular at first. I knew however from a friend that my old patterns could occur to an increased extent, so that it was better to stay at home, which I did. After approximately three hours I went through a total negative phase. I called my best friend, who

116

got the full benefit. Fortunately I had warned Alexandra in advance. Old patterns of a senseless life and suicide thoughts came up again. I saw many things a lot more negatively than they actually are. This went on for about one day; then the negative feelings disappeared and for two days I had so much energy like never before in my life. I was literally glowing from the inside out. On these two days I worked late into the night and only went to bed at 7:30 in the morning, tired, but very content. I wish for all people to experience this energy!

•

It's unbelievable, dear Martin: it is 8 p.m. on the last day of the holidays – and not one lesson is prepared (tomorrow I have eight hours on three different subjects), and still I don't feel this paralysing, gagging pressure!! On the contrary, I can laugh about it, I feel positive and carefree!!!

Haven't felt like that for a long time!

Well done to both of us, S.

•

Hello!

After having participated in one of Martin's healing seminars and heard of his healing school during that evening, I felt the strong desire to attend the school. I also told my friend of that evening, as it had helped to relieve my chronic earache, and this encouraged me to enrol us both. The first days were very hard for me personally. I had slept very little on the day before the journey, as I was suffering from a terrible cough which kept me awake at night up until midweek. I felt that the fire ceremony on the first evening took forever and I could barely sing because my voice went. In comparison

I found working with the other participants very stimulating. Although many of us had no idea what we were doing there, something seemed to loosen up in all participants. Most of all I enjoyed the comfortable atmosphere after the opening of the holy room, and thought that the evening on which the seeing rights were entrusted to us was particularly impressive. I have always been sensitive and somewhat perceptive, but I haven't been able to interpret these gifts properly, let alone use them. After Martin had entrusted me with these rights I suddenly saw many wonderful images of old buildings and plants, which complemented the background music very nicely. It was as if a door to a new world had been opened.

The bestowal of the protective ribbons was also lovely. Martin's assistants seemed like angels and the mood was very reverent. When I woke up on the following morning the effect of the ribbons made itself felt already. I saw how something dark fell on me from above, but when it hit my luminous body it bounced back, unable to enter.

On Thursday, after all my issues, as we had specified them at the beginning of the course, had been successfully cleared and my heart chakra was feeling considerably lighter, I finally had my cough treated. My shaman told me afterwards that he had seen a girl working in a field despite the rain and cold; she was suffering from a bad cough. The issue behind the energy blockade that manifested itself as a cough seemed therefore to originate from an earlier life – on the following day the cough had disappeared completely.

During an exercise at which we were to observe nature, I also discovered that I can talk with nature, and during the second fire ceremony I had the feeling of becoming one with the fire. I didn't feel the cold or my tiredness, and after the ceremony all the participants felt they were able to see "more light" in the darkness.

The first few weeks after the Foundation course it seemed to me that I was rediscovering the world from scratch. I felt as if I was constantly shedding my skin like a snake and becoming more open; on some days I did feel the desire to just stay in bed and see nobody, but after I had got over this phase I perceived myself and my environment as much brighter, lighter and more cheerful. The course turned many things into positives and also strengthened the bond between my boyfriend and me.

When we argue now we don't lose ourselves in accusations anymore; we ask each other which issue could lie behind our respective reaction and then do a clearing. Because due to these clearings great changes occurred inside me, I found them as very fatiguing, even shortly after the course. Meanwhile I have come to enjoy every clearing and am glad for being able to support my fellow human beings with the help of the spirits.

My boyfriend and I have now set up a dedicated room for clearings, where all the elements and energy animals are represented.

Petra

Dear Martin

I've slept without woolly socks on for two nights now, keep your fingers crossed that it continues. Apart from that I'm in quite a speedy mood, floating a little bit (otherwise I would never write such a mail).

Best regards J.

Hello Herr Brune,

In early March I had my telephone consultation with you. My main issue was the relationship with my ex-wife, which doesn't seem to want to end. Our regular arguments and discussions deeply upset and agitated me, both privately and professionally. Now, five weeks later, our arguing has reduced greatly, and most importantly, it preoccupies me only on a practical level and doesn't upset me as much anymore. You also worked on my third chakra. I can now say that since then I find a lot of things easier, and that things that had come to a halt for a long time are now making progress again. For this I would like to express my gratitude.

With kind regards

Thomas

•

Hi Martin,
    Thank you for your mail.
    …some thinking principles have changed in my mind. Since we've been working together I find it easier to live and let live, and this makes my team happy, of course.
    See you later. Yours sincerely R.
    Hello Martin,
    It is great that you replied so swiftly!
    I feel that I have to thank you for yesterday, for letting me share your knowledge and your work. I felt there was no proper opportunity to tell you that personally yesterday …
    I found the combination of yoga and shamanic work particularly appealing, as both have been accompanying me in

my life for a long time. For that reason I was aware of and familiar with several things and didn't feel inadequate in any way. Kind regards, C.

•

Hello Martin,

I have been reviewing the time since the first course. Perhaps you can find something here that can be useful to you...

For a very long time I've often had situations in which I thought I was going mad. I found books that exactly describe my experiences and things were ok again. On the other hand, I didn't talk to anyone about it. Although my visions always lasted only moments, it was enough for me!! And so it went on and on.

Yet it would never have occurred to me to seek the help of a shaman. My "natural" defences were stopping me, I thought they were all nutcases. But then...

At the seminars, suddenly everything fell into place, including the noises. My "craziness" was so normal here that everything felt crazy again. Switching off the intellect is not so simple!

I experienced a lot, particularly in the second seminar. Very old issues became clear. From an understanding point of view this had already been clear to me for a long time, as I work in life counselling with emphasis on the "inner child" and text meditations for letting go. However, another totally new quality came to light: hatred. This intensity was absolutely new and strange to me and yet known. My shaman did a great job in one session and removed a possession, which she described to me in total consistence with my issues. I was flabbergasted. And it has really done me good to be rid of it. To this day! A lot of things have changed. Almost like a new life. Above all I can see a lot more clearly what my interests/desires are, and what effect others have on me. Where to adopt things from.

In my work with clients I have gradually stopped being surprised or amazed. I simply trust. And contrary to my other occupational activity, this work does not fatigue me. With one client I had five sessions and at the end she said "wow, I looked through my notes, we've worked on all the emotions". She was astonished – the circle had closed completely. She could now tread new paths and during the final session we had one of these "holy moments", where just peace and gratitude prevail. Another client was affected by a very strong inner anxiety. She was no longer able to switch off and felt like a bundle of energy. When I looked into her energy, I saw a huge swarm of hornets which kept the original energy going. There was also a very cheerful mood there, exactly the same as she was feeling at that moment. The energy changed and she was able to breathe deeply and calmly. Over the following days she popped in regularly to report how balanced she now felt.

With another client we worked on her helplessness as regards "bullying". She wrote a few weeks later and thanked me for the session, as she could now deal with the situation in a completely different manner. One client had lost her son and went to see a shaman in the Amazon (not that this would have put me under pressure *grin*). Her son had wanted to work in an aid project there and she then supported this project in his name. Before our session she dreamed about him. During the session I could see the connection/the energy.

The energy left lovingly (if one can call it that) and went to the light. The pain went and gratitude remained. She kept trying to go back to the pain over the next few days, but she couldn't feel it anymore.

If you like, you're welcome to use any of this input.

Best regards and happy Easter

Sabine

•

Hello Martin

J. was still in very good spirits yesterday. This morning, when he had to do the rest of his homework, we had a bit of a setback again. First he said "the session with this man yesterday did nothing at all". In the course of doing his homework, however, he recovered really well, which is not necessarily always the case, and finished his stuff in relative peace and quite independently.

A good evening to you, see you tomorrow. P.

•

Hello Martin,

I would be pleased if I could contribute to your work and am sending you some case reports, from which you could choose the fitting ones for your book.

I had a lady for hand-surgical aftercare, who, after a complicated wrist fracture, had developed Morbus Sudeck in treatment. Conventional medicine has so far been unable to determine the cause of this very painful and lengthy follow-up illness.

Frau A. could not use her work hand and consequently not pursue her occupation any longer, which exerted additional psychological pressure. After two energetic healings the Morbus Sudeck disappeared. Frau A. required some physiotherapy for a short period of time in order to regain the restrictions of movement resulting from the M.S.

The mother of an 11-year-old boy with ADD (attention deficit disorder with no hyperactivity = dreamer syndrome) asked for an appointment for energetic healing treatment. She told me that her son P. had been suffering from sleep disorders since his birth, and that they intensified when he'd started school.

P. would wake up nearly each night crying and screaming. As a result, he went to school tired every morning and was not able to follow the classes despite normal intelligence. He constantly forgot important things which were needed at school, or didn't know what homework he had to do. The tense situation also had an effect on the family harmony.

When P. was eight years old, his parents decided to pursue a therapy with drugs, whose only success was that P. lost his childlike nature completely and became almost depressed. Thereupon his mother discontinued the drug.

Since an energetic healing treatment, in which some blockades that were very strongly manifested in his energy field were detected and removed, P. has been sleeping through the night without interruption, according to his mother. He goes to school feeling refreshed, is wide awake and can follow the lessons attentively. His marks have clearly improved and he will certainly manage the syllabus in secondary school. Ok, Martin, that's it. Kind regards Gabi.

•

Hallo Martin,

vida loca is good… hits the nail on the head. I'd like to come on Monday morning. See you then, love A.

•

Hello Martin,

Sometimes I spontaneously tell people during the massage treatment in the hotel about the shamanic method of healing and they arrange an appointment with me. This was the case with a pleasant lady from abroad who told me that she was the publisher of a major Home & Living lifestyle magazine. Her issue was that she was afraid of being photographed, be it for the magazine or for any other reason. She always felt unphotogenic on her own pictures. In recent years she has developed a real aversion to it, which has also become a burden in other situations in life.

During the session a deep healing in the second chakra occurred, which was accompanied by an indescribable merriness and a deep gratitude. When she opened her eyes again 30 minutes later, I noticed that her whole facial expression had changed. Her cheeks were gleaming rosy and the individual features looked more refined and more good-natured. Her entire manner seemed much warmer and more vigorous. With an inner luminosity she looked at me and said with tears in her eyes: "I cannot believe it! I feel beautiful for the first time in my life."

A month later she sent me the latest issue of her magazine with a picture of her on the front cover and a wide enchanting smile.

Frank Herrmann
  White Stone Lounge
  Frankfurt
  Hi Martin,
I have a totally different feeling to people around me, for example to my colleagues yesterday. I no longer feel so small and – yes – the neediness is gone, that's probably it. I'm also discovering a totally different relationship to the environment, I really enjoy walking during the day in any weather, but recently also in the middle at the night through the dark forest, that was great. A.

•

Dear Martin and Conny,
  I'd like to write a few lines on my experiences so far during and after the Foundation seminar.

At the beginning of the seminar I was at first rather reserved and sometimes also sceptical, particularly with the rituals. Gradually however I noticed that something heavy and oppressive fell off me, something that I had been feeling since my childhood days.

I discovered abilities in me, which up until then I hadn't been aware of in this shape. Since that time I have been feeling more inspired and a deeper connection with the "great spirit". I was amazed when, after an exercise with another participant, she told me that I had "seen" and described aspects from her life so accurately that she felt embarrassed at first.

One day later however she told me how glad she was to have finally come into contact with these issues in a new way; she felt much lighter and happier after we had worked on these issues. I would not have thought that I could be able to look so deeply so quickly with a "simple" exercise. It showed me once again that at the end we are all ONE. Having the privilege of seeing the inner pictures of the energy centres and following how they gradually turn into positive while working on them is something I find very precious and healing, for both people.

Since that time I have been implementing this work into my practice too, and I show and say more courageously what I perceive. In the beginning it felt somewhat strange using the rattle in order to be able to see the inner pictures clearer and call the spirit, but after a few days it was perfectly alright. People accept it and report of their own perceptions afterwards, during the "reading" and "treating" of the energy centres. Dear Martin, thank you for this kind of seeing. I look forward to further, more in-depth seminars.

Ok, this is my contribution.

I am sending you Easter wishes and look forward to the next seminar. Love Agnes

•

Hello, for two years I have had trouble with energies which stream into me and are not mine. They rob my strength from me, provoke substantial fears and threaten my basic existence. The physical effects are as follows: in the evening I go to bed at 21:00 completely exhausted, but my sleep doesn't seem to be restful. I feel as if I have stayed awake all night. Last summer my body developed a cold allergy. It is incredible how a light breeze causes my skin to go cold. My skin reacts with burning, goes red, glows as if I had sunburn and swells up. Acute pains in the left side of my chest come and go and are under examination. Perhaps they are muscular.

In autumn 2005 I developed fears that forced me to take on tasks that demand too much of me: three jobs and a honorary chairmanship. These fears were replaced by others that distress me even more; strange ideas disturb my thoughts permanently. I feel very unwell, almost dirty. I am infinitely sad and don't know why. I smoke and drink, I am very anxious, stressed and visit a pilgrimage church regularly.

For some months now I've had something in my left ear, I hear noises, sounds, a hiss as from a radio. I suddenly have the feeling that I am not alone, that two dead people hold me by the shoulders, one on the left and one on the right. They are my grandfather, whom I never met, and a good friend of mine.

My physician is an anthroposophist, he accompanies and supports me – he recommended that I went to a family constellation seminar. In the constellation I found that I must return something that is irresolvable and belongs to my grandfather. The therapist says it is high time for me to do something, I am in danger.

I am not supposed to fight these fears, because then I will apparently open the door to them! I feel like withdrawing, don't like meeting other people. I spend my time thinking, take up piano again, begin a patchwork course, go to martial arts training again, work in the garden, go jogging, meditate and try to be in the here and now.

I read Rudolf Meyer's "The meaning of suffering and the development of inner life", my suffering accelerates my development process, brilliant.

One of the participants at the constellation seminar remarked that my topics could perhaps be dealt with shamanism. I investigated and came across the Shamanic Healing Institute. I read the report by Martin Brune and saw from the website that long-distance treatments are possible and without further ado I asked for an appointment. I was very agitated and anxious – but what could be worse than what I go through every day?

At the appointed time I called; I was a nervous wreck, had trouble specifying three issues. Herr Brune took in my sadness at first, I should breathe into the telephone, then put the phone down and lie down. What happened to me then is unbelievable! I felt wave-like movements in my lower abdomen which caused a contraction in the abdominal muscles, my upper body reared up – I felt alone and sadness overcame me, I hyperventilated, although I know that I shouldn't. My respiratory system felt very strange, I felt as if I had died several times. My body breathed out until there was nothing more left, again and again, sometimes deeply and sometimes stertorously. Although my eyes were closed I could perceive darkness and light. Cold flowed through my body and pulled me to the ground. Then I was a wild animal snarling, digging into the ground. Wavelike movements kept rising from the lower to the upper abdomen, my upper body reared up, my mouth opened and a breath rushed out. I felt more and more relieved. This infinite sadness had dissipated. I felt good.

The second hour was different: now I was predominantly an animal that snarls and hisses. Then I was someone who is oddly bad and full of scorn. My respiration was accompanied by groaning and screaming. Towards the end I was more relaxed. I felt good.

The third hour is pending. It will surely be exciting. The therapist's as well as my doctor's advice is that I absolutely must ground myself! How am I supposed to ground myself, I am already here on Earth? I am to draw myself but can only draw myself incompletely!

The assessment of the sessions is interesting, but since I have little idea about shamanism, it's not much good to me. Perhaps it is not even necessary. However, I have now found some literature that should help me to understand. I have the feeling that I should deal with it beyond the sessions. Thank you again, Petra

•

"My issue with men …"

Throughout my whole life, and I am now 34, I've had a timorous and odd relationship to men. Relationships have always been extremely difficult and loaded with problems, full of fears of "letting in" and "being dropped". From an early age on I would walk with my shoulders rounded and my head down when was I alone, trying to avoid being recognized as a girl.

Irrational fear – but of what? No idea! It actually wasn't that I was totally isolated and kept clear of all men, no! On the contrary, I would launch myself into a new relationship, always hoping that from now on everything would be different! But every time it ended in disaster, with tears, love-sickness or endless discussions. Did I love? Yes I did! But differently than today.

To me, love was associated with pain. But I can only see this clearly today, upon reflection. In addition my life was marked by restless nights, panic attacks from a certain age onward, also at night, and: almost every night at about one o'clock I was visited by a man whose face I could not make out, but his shape was all the more menacing for that reason. For many years, I didn't really think much about it,

"Nightmares, right – everyone has them sometime. You're just overanxious...". But still these nocturnal "visits" wore me out and I was always tired. At the same time my panic attacks intensified whenever a new "partner" was at my side at night. Interesting! At least with hindsight....

On a Shamanic Healing seminar by Martin Brune in Cologne, about which I heard from my brother, I, among all the participants, was given a demo "healing session", and – there are no coincidences – that was the beginning of the end for my issue with men!

No less than two shamans worked on me and described to me the most interesting images! After that I had another session a week later, which did not only give me information concerning my fears but brought about a groundbreaking change in my life. Martin did a soul retrieval and told me of pictures that were not at all strange to me, and which somehow must have been buried under the surface – except at night! Everything fitted together and a previous life explained my situation in this one! But the best thing is that since that session I've not had one fear attack, the "visits" are over and the culmination is:

Martin said we should wait to see what happens, because things could also change in my intimate relationships with men. As a matter of fact, exactly four weeks later I met a man on holiday who was totally different to all the others I'd met before. For the first time in my life I have a relationship which is evenly matched and without "stress".

For the first time I am involved with someone without fear and enjoy all the aspects of the relationship. This is completely new to me! And yet it came just like that, without me having to change anything in ME. In a transferred sense one could say that one affected the other unconsciously. Of course, this can only be seen afterwards. Everything is connected, everything has a cause. Two sessions changed my life. That much is certain. I can't wait to see what is still to come – but today I know that sometimes everything finds an explanation! Many many thanks, Wibke

•

Hello Martin,

As far I as I can think back in this life my awareness of life has consisted exclusively of a mixture of shame, fear and inadequacy. I was ashamed of myself, felt unloved and was afraid to speak, afraid of people, of life, of everything. When I was a child I was only vaguely aware of it. Once I asked a friend in primary school whether she also suffered from these feelings and she said no. I was surprised and full of envy. I always had friends, but as soon as I had more than five people around me I felt anxious and wouldn't dare to speak. In eighth grade I stayed down a year because I didn't say one word in any of the classes.

At the age of around sixteen I became fully aware of my inner situation. I began to reflect, found explanations and recognized that my condition was not "normal", or better: "natural". When I reached twenty I decided to do a conversation-based therapy – a difficult undertaking for someone like me! The therapy did not help; it confused me and made me feel even more unsure than I already was.

Parallel to that I devoured the books of Castaneda and other authors about their experiences with shamans – their world seemed unattainable for me. It involved healing, transcendence and liberty: simply wonderful!

One day a friend actually gave me the address of a shaman in my town. I couldn't believe it! I was innerly overjoyed! My confidence was greater than my fear. On the same day – it was Easter Sunday(!) – I called her. Through our work together I experienced for the first time a real inner change. Healing processes were noticeable on all levels. Parallel to that, similar abilities seemed to develop within me. Having finished my training as a teacher, it was clear that my path should follow that direction. But how?

One day I was surfing the Internet for books, when suddenly an announcement of Martin's healing school flashed on the screen. I followed the link and had tears of joy streaming down my face. I knew that this was the way to go. But how could I possibly afford it? I didn't have a job, had no possessions – I was just saving to buy a kettle. Finally a friend gave me the money and I booked the first training course.

"No one has to live up to themselves here", Martin said once during the course and I smiled innerly, because I knew that this was exactly the reason I was there. The work during that week was simple, clear and direct –without the aloof spiritual atmosphere. Martin was very strong and under his guidance we became both healers and healed – each at their own speed. I wasn't the only one to be full of gratitude when I saw how simply and efficiently the techniques that Martin gave us functioned.

I drove home with new self-assurance and full of strength. There I was surprised to find out that my plants were suddenly talking to me. They were asking for water and my rubber plant acted as if it was ticklish when I sprayed it.

I wanted to put my knowledge into practice immediately. My first client was my shaman. More followed and with each one of them I realised that I had actually become a channel towards healing.

For my first fire ritual (coursework) I stood alone in the darkness in a quarry. Eerie noises were coming from everywhere – I was frightened. After I had opened the holy room, the smell of Martin's scented water (he uses it for the healings) flew past my chest and took my fear with it...

... a wonderful story with a quick happy ending? Unfortunately not! While I am writing this report, I find myself again in deep, dark confusion. There is no way at the moment for me to realise my dream of a small shamanic practice. I am shaken by existential fear. Nobody comes to be treated, so there are no prospects for a regular job or income. What is the matter? Was it all just the evil product of a euphoric faith, an illusion, fed by hope? No.

I can only face this deeper layer of fear with which I am confronted at the moment because of the work we've done. For at the same time I feel, even if only fleetingly but still more fundamentally, a confidence in the existence which will point the way to me. Meanwhile I continue to work on my fear and on my grounding.

The journey on the shamanic path continues; it leads me in a spiral, through the dark areas into ever greater freedom. The provisions for the journey consist of increasing zest for life, love and confidence. The luggage that is lost on the way is only what we wanted to lose anyway. I am happy for everyone who enters this way! Daniela

•

Hello,

I have been busying myself with energy work for a long time. However, after reading a book on the healing techniques of the Inca shamans, I really wanted to know more about this kind of healing and did some research on the Internet, where I finally found the homepage of the "Shamanic Healing Institute". The short seminar with the shamanic healing journey aroused my interest immediately and I enrolled for the next date, which was two weeks later.

When Martin began to speak about this healing method, I immediately knew that this was exactly what I was missing in order to fulfil my heart's desire: to help others as well as myself. I just had to learn this healing method.

The next foundation seminar was in one month's time and I was determined to take part, but where should I get the money for it from? Some days later I had the necessary money available and could finally enrol for the seminar. I could hardly wait for it to begin.

Then the day finally came, I was very much looking forward to the seminar, but when I began to pack my things into the car, a feeling of fear and doubt suddenly descended on me. I asked myself that I was doing here, why should I spend so much money on such a course, and was considering whether I should drive there at all. Despite these feelings I got into the car and drove off with an uneasy feeling in my stomach. The further I drove away from home the better I felt, and I began again to look forward to the seminar. Yet the fear didn't leave me completely. Fear of what I was in for and particularly of all the other people who would be participating in the seminar.

After arriving at the beautiful villa Schaaffhausen, despite my initial doubts I immediately felt comfortable with the people in my group, some of whom I had already met at lunch. The seminar was to begin at 14:00. I was to introduce myself in front of all these strangers. That had always been my greatest problem at school and my heart was beating like mad. Among other things I made this fear the issue of the first clearing. During the clearing process I saw beautiful colours and afterwards my chakra felt as if someone had built a fan in it. It was a lighter, freer feeling. When, later, we were to report of our experiences before the group, I surprised myself by volunteering to share what I had experienced with the others without thinking. In fact, I was happy to do it.

I thought that the other clearings would be probably just as gentle and looked forward to finally getting rid of my fears.

The next clearings, particularly the third and the fourth, were very, very intensive. I felt as if my arms and legs were chained to the floor, I was unable to move and felt this strong tingling in my arms and legs. When the tingling finally subsided and I could feel my arms and legs again, the sensation was beautiful. I finally felt free. It was a feeling of liberation like I had never felt it before in my life. A feeling as if someone had removed the chains that had kept me fettered and had been cutting into my flesh all that time. I was just happy.

The last day of the seminar came much too quickly. I didn't want to go home yet, I just wanted to get rid of everything, completely everything. Besides I had very much taken to our group. The energy that prevailed between us was simply wonderful. The last clearing however – I was already prepared for another very intensive experience – ran very serenely. I just felt how everything that did not belong to me left my body and felt very good.

Also the ceremonies we experienced in the evenings during the seminar were beautiful and very moving. These were truly very moving experiences, which everyone should experience for themselves.

I am happy not to have missed one day of this wonderful, intensive week and am very grateful that I was allowed to experience all that. I have already enrolled for the seeing course and look forward to it with nervous anticipation. Love, Kerstin

Hello Martin!

First of all I am overjoyed that I discovered this seminar on the Internet by coincidence and attended it. I benefited a lot from that day. I was without pain for five days. I still think of that day often and about how I could continue, because I want to finally get rid of these bone metastases. Uwe

•

Hi Martin,

The session last Thursday was very effective. I had a seminar at the weekend and it was clearly noticeable that I was lot more concentrated than before. I no longer had the need to withdraw into my inner self. I was able to involve myself in the requirements and was almost permanently present. It is a feeling of being released and being able to act, and it is a very important step forward, as it gets exactly to the heart of the matter.

The overall situation is still exactly the same, only it is substantially toned down now. The feeling of being attacked by certain things still arises occasionally. But now I do not lose myself in it anymore; I manage to maintain the perspective. I can withstand it better now and not let the bottom drop out of my world so fast. It is as if the volume had been turned down noticeably.

I can't wait to see what will happen in the future. Hopefully the development will continue in the same direction, so that I will be free of doubt and stand firmly on my feet.

Thanks for the help, Marco

•

Hello Martin, hello Conny,

I left with a peculiar and relaxed feeling yesterday. On the drive home I first had the impulse to cry again and later to laugh. In fact I walked through the railway station grinning. Everything settled a little and I was relaxed and tired. I wanted to say something regarding the picture of the frozen man. It could have been my grandfather who died when I was about 13 years old. I can still remember clearly that he gave me his hand on the night before he died, and I knew that this was a farewell and he was going to die. However I can't remember having spoken to someone at that moment or directly afterwards. When I told a friend about it today I had to cry again. Moreover, my granddad was afraid of illness. I also remember having a dream not long after his death, in which I stand on the stairs and he (looking healthy) looks at me with a concentrated expression on his face, doesn't say anything though and goes back into his bedroom, the room in which he died.

I was feeling well this morning and couldn't wait to share the experience with a friend. I also felt relaxed, but that changed toward the evening, when I started feeling an inner restlessness and an urge to do something, without knowing the direction. However in some situations I was more relaxed than before and certainly had a prevailing mood of positiveness today. I somehow have the feeling that it still works, but can't explain it any clearer. Now while I'm writing this and think about the day I also feel a light pain around my heart or a pressure on the chest again….

Ok, I think that was it.

Many thanks, it definitely was a valuable experience.
Regards Nicole

•

Hi Martin,

There is already an effect perceptible from the session yesterday. What came into my consciousness is the fear of not becoming healthy again. My will to be healed is great and I have decided to do everything within my power to achieve this. The problem was only that I was always trying to have everything run according to my conceptions. This had led to the fact that my self (the lower self) had to carry a much too heavy load, because it then thinks it has to, or can, change things, over which it does not possess any power. Thus it refuses to accept the natural flow and takes on an unsupportable task.

Now it becomes clear that the self should abandon itself to the flow of things (the higher self), no matter what happens after. Because whether the healing is done or not now – this is the only possibility to untie myself from the causes of the disease. The point here is to untie myself form the old context and adapt myself to a new one. Only then will the things happen that can happen, that are possible. This breaking-free has not been possible for me to achieve so far and has led to a total hardening and ossification. At the same time, a feeling of pressure exists, a sense of being locked up and of a weight that rests on me from the outside and robs me of the possibility to move. This is the case on all levels of the self, and it unfortunately also affects the body. My only doubts concern the recovery of the body, the inner dimensions seem to be able to change more easily. The body (seemingly) puts up obstacles and therefore I find it difficult to become friends with it. I am becoming increasingly aware of this and that triggers a feeling of relief and aliveness. Hopefully it can continue in the same way – during the good phases I am quite self-assured and have confidence.

Many thanks for your help! Marco

•

Hello Martin,

I was at your last healing journey in Vienna in 2005 and am writing this to say thank you again for your help.

I have left my old fears behind me and know that my path goes in the shamanic direction (and although I have known it for my whole life, now is the right time for me to give it some serious thought).

Many many thanks for accompanying me along this path.

Kind regards from Vienna
from Heide

•

Hello Martin,

As promised, I am sending you the following feedback:

On the same evening of the long-distance healing session I was overcome by existential fears, which I had not experienced in this magnitude for a long time. There I also realised suddenly what you meant with "issue". Believe me, the next time I will certainly be able to name my issue. In addition I felt physically very exhausted for almost a week. Today, my fears are still there, though in an abated form, thank God, and physically I feel considerably lighter. On the exterior, for the first time in years I have applied for a job which I would really like to do very much. So I firmly believe in a miracle at Christmas.

In this spirit I wish you and Anja merry Christmas, a relaxing festive season and a happy new year.

Love from stormy Vienna
Daniela

Basic glossary of energy medicine

Chakra. Sanskrit for "wheel of light". There exist countless books of all mystery schools about chakras. About how they look, how they work, which colour they are or what characteristics they possess, and even about which illnesses are associated with them. I didn't want to write a new book about chakras. To me, chakras are spinning energy centres – no more and no less. Any association of a chakra with an illness, a colour, or a characteristic is very western: it may be logical, but is not really appropriate. The cause of a problem in the stomach could just as well be an energy disturbance in the heart chakra. These associations are confusing, and that's why I am not adopting them.

Energy. For shamans, energy is simply "light". The fourth element in nature next to body, soul and mind. Apart from that it is difficult to define energy in itself. The other elements are classically treated by medicine (body), psychology (soul) and science (mind). The vague concept of energy has led to the strong suppression of energy as a healing topic by the mystery schools of Christianity and the scientific world view. Only psychoanalysis and its method of the interpretation of dreams as well as Sigmund Freud's research on rites in other cultures have brought up again the possibility of employing "different" aspects of healing. In spiritual medicine EVERY symptom, every illness, whether physical or psychological, is treated as an energetic imbalance, without the elimination of which the true source of the problem has not been healed.

Energy medicine. By energy medicine we understand a spiritual medicine that heals with the help of light.

Envisioning. Fulfilment of our vision, of our life's dream, of our life contract. Contrary to our western culture, the issue of illness occupies only a minor significance in shamanic tradition. Illnesses are ->manifestations of energy disturbances, and these are easily healed. A lengthy consideration of illness is absent from shamanic culture, as the main task in our life is the "cultivation of our field", the realisation of our life's dream, of our visions. In the third course of the Energy School students learn to energetically "get" their life's dream with the help of energy techniques.

Mind. In this context the mind is what permanently tries to find out (mostly by pondering) why we feel unwell. In our western world, among other things, we use the mind in the hope to solve our problems. The level of the mind is totally superfluous in the context of healing (as a client). For a shaman the mind is important for the formulation of intent.

Intent. Intent has its origin in the mind but is equipped with an energy which at some point ->manifests itself on the exterior. (Everyone knows the parking lot exercise, in which one wishes to find a parking space).

Intuition. Intuition is a feeling which sometimes has no rational grounds but proves to be correct later. Confidence in our own intuition is what all of us have nearly lost. In the context of energetic medicine, the students of the Energy School learn to leave their life in the hands of the natural powers, their own intuition. Intuition then guides us to make the right decisions in life.

Body. The body is the physical body.

Light. Energy. Where darkness prevails, there is illness.

Manifestation, to be manifested. In this context it means "to become visible" in reality. An energy disturbance, for instance, can manifest itself as an illness. Or also become evident in the circumstances in which we live. Deficient thinking, the wrong partner, etc. are manifestations of energy disturbances.

Shaman. "Medium between worlds" – the real and the energetic worlds. A social authority, roughly combining the functions of a priest and a doctor in one, also known as "medicine man" or "medium". The shaman draws his knowledge from the traditional culture of ->shamanism that has been handed down over the centuries, and heals by ->seeing, removing dark stains – the energy disturbances in the energy field – and bundling energies.

Shamanism. Comes from "shaman" (from the Siberian Turkic languages) and means "spiritual healing". The term shamanism has been moulded by many mystery schools, movements and people.

Soul. In this context the soul is the sphere of emotions (fears, depression, grief, and so on).

Seeing. "Seeing energies" is the ability a shaman must learn in order to be able to find symptoms in the shape of dark stains (energy disturbances) in the luminous energy field of the client. With the use of other techniques, the student in the Energy School learns to activate the self-healing powers of the client.

Vision. Vision is the life's dream, the fulfilment of the life contract with which we were born.

The Energy School

The notion of being able to say goodbye to our entire life's burdens, our dramas and our traumas, just dispose of them once and for all and look forward, is a beautiful one. If we don't do that we will carry with us kilos of dirty laundry on the raft of our life stream. And when the laundry gets soaked with water we will sometimes go under.

Therefore we shouldn't fool ourselves. We must first throw our ballast overboard, clean ourselves, and this will only work if we are prepared to look deeply into our wounds in order to transform these into sources of power. That means work in itself. But this work is not associated with results or achievement; only with recognizing and being aware of our own problems, turning them in to an "issue" and then have the wound healed.

And it is these sources that will drive the raft full speed ahead towards our destiny, towards happiness and self-realisation. Every obstacle will be worked on, every heavy stone will be dealt with and removed. Until we reach maximum speed...

The obstacles are the problems we haven't dealt with, traumas, past conflicts, apologies never expressed, our difficult childhood, our brother, father, sister, the dramas with our mother. All these energies inform and determine our everyday life still today. How are we to attain our destiny, our self-realisation, if we don't get rid of the heap of dirty laundry and the rocks in the river?

The Energy School is called Energy School because it is not merely a seeing or healing school. The school imparts old energetic knowledge that helps to open up our future.

For we shouldn't waste our life dealing with illness – the field of our life needs to be cultivated now. This is about our dreams. It is about our happiness. Not the happiness offered by formulas for happiness and counsellors, but the fulfilment of our life's dream that is in our life contract. It is about making happiness possible to experience as such, not just claiming we are happy but really feeling it.

Everyone can learn the energy techniques. Here, too, the reports of success are outstanding. I have learned to steer what I thought was suffering and finally discovered to be power – and others can simply study and practice it. This Energy School merely follows in the path our archaic, pre-Christian cultures trod, in which everyone healed everyone or consulted a shaman. How else can the fact be explained that shamanism exists from Siberia to Cape Horn?

Turning our world view upside down

The school is structured on three main courses, which can be covered within approximately one year. In order to be able to live our dream liberated from inherited problems, we must first become "pure".

Clearing: Foundation Course

The techniques to do this are taught in the Foundation Course. The students here learn to let go of the past not "with their head" but rather by working on it energetically and eliminating it.

Participants are often surprised how easily and quickly symptoms such as fear or tinnitus disappear. Without psychotherapy. Without drugs. Simply by blowing into a stone and working with a shaman. That's all it takes.

Many processes in this energy medicine are different, as I often say. In this energy medicine we "heal" first by eliminating the energy imbalance.

Act before you think:
Heal first, understand later.

Only days later will the client understand how the symptom came about. Most traditional therapy methods are aimed at understanding everything first. And only once we have understood everything could we then heal. Here it is the exact opposite: first comes the healing, then the understanding.

The example of Judy from Los Angeles makes this clear: Judy said she had the urge to scratch her face all the time, and couldn't explain why. She didn't know why. She had seen many psychologists and non-medical practitioners – all to no avail.

In the second chakra I saw in her luminous energy field a male possession, which had treated her very badly when she was a little girl. The treatment led this possession to the light. One week later Judy reported that she couldn't believe it, but she hadn't scratched her face once since.

A month later she wrote a mail, in which she accounted that she had been raped when she was a child and had started scratching her face afterwards to make herself uglier and less attractive. This "came" from her one week ago. She realised that this was the reason for her scratching – not neurodermatitis or severe self-hatred.

In the Foundation Course the students learn to find and work on energy disturbances in the luminous energy field of the client. This is the Clearing process.

Minor energies and heavy energies can be eliminated through this process. Practical exercises take up eighty percent of the time of the entire course. The students learn to heal themselves as well as others and to eliminate their own wounds; they begin to work on and clear up the river of their life.

That is the reason why the school is so interesting for everyone: because most people carry with them many burdens from their past.

See with your heart: Seeing Course

In the Seeing Course the students learn to see, if they haven't learned it yet in the Foundation Course. During an initiation, I open and clean the third eye of the student.

"Seeing" is the most misunderstood word. Most people associate with "seeing" the ability to see fantastically coloured auras, a firework of light surrounding the client, or similar fantastic ideas. All that is NOT seeing. "Seeing" in shamanic tradition rather means to see not only with your eyes, but also with your heart. It means to learn to see behind the surface, behind the mask of the client. It means to learn to see the true stories behind the energy disturbances. And "seeing" can indeed mean to see, but also to taste, smell or just feel. "Seeing" is all that.

After successful consultations students often report that they saw not only the trauma in the shape of pictures but also smelled the scent of the scenery and heard the ambient noises. All that means to see „energy". The pure aura-seeing is only a small part of what the student learns in the school.

Many experienced students of other shamanic schools come to us in order to learn to see. For only when one can really see can one extract energies, be it possessions which must be led to the light or just heavy energy in the shape of arrows, swords or knives, and eliminate them successfully from the client's luminous energy field. I have personally visited several other shamanic schools. Only few of the people who had completed their courses could really extract, as they were not able to really „see".

The essential techniques for the extraction of energies are also a component of the Seeing Course. What use would it be to the client if we could see the energies but couldn't remove them?

Many clients come to us at the institute because they have been told by „seers" or fortune tellers that they carry a possession inside them or they have experienced something very bad in an earlier life.

„So", we often ask, „why did they send you home with it?"

We will only send a client home after the energies have been removed. Because the students learn not only to see but also to remove the dark stains. And where darkness disappears the space is filled by light.

The client hears the history of what the shaman has seen only at the end of the consultation. By then the energy blockades have been extracted, and the history belongs to the past. As far as his/her issue is concerned, the client goes home pure, and can relax and forget about everything.

The Seeing Course is a very popular course; it is booked both by the participants of the Foundation Course and by participants of other schools. Another reason is the course's second part, in which students learn the immensely important soul retrieval. Soul retrieval is basically the reclamation of life energy which was lost at some point in the past, maybe even hundreds of years ago (the sceptics among you will probably roll their eyes now). The reclaiming of this natural and essential life energy can work wonders. I know from my practical experience that the most complex issues can be healed through soul retrieval.

The Seeing Course is all that. At the end of the course, the students learn to treat each other over the telephone. Most of the students are awed by this technique – especially when the success of the treatment is confirmed afterwards by the person they treated. The feedback is sensational. If one could record it all, it would really be the material films are made of.

All students can see energies after the Seeing Course. There hasn't been one student of our school who couldn't master that at the end of the course. I am so absolutely convinced of the quality of the training that I often let my students treat me.

After the Seeing Course the students have control of all the techniques necessary for energetically healing each other, from energies from this life as well as from energies from previous lives. So the students feel safe. Very safe. Because they know that they can heal one another from a distance, as all they need to do is call a fellow student on the phone and arrange a long-distance consultation. No one feels alone anymore. There are enough shamans one can work with, so physical distance is no longer a barrier if one has a problem that needs to be treated.

Find your life contract: Envisioning

All of that, however, actually serves one purpose only: the preparation for what is yet to come. In the Envisioning Course the students learn to deal with the reason why we actually are in this world. They learn to use their ability to shape their world in order to finally fulfil their life contract, their calling in the form of self-realisation.

The central characteristic of the Envisioning Course is the energetic extraction of ALL this that really holds us back from realising our calling. The energetic work of the Foundation and the Seeing Courses only serve to cleanse and prepare ourselves. In the Envisioning Course we principally "jump" into the fresh adventurous water of our life.

I would like to invite everyone to share this experience.

Note:

On our website http://www.shamanic.de/ you can find extensive information on the work of Martin Brune, the Energy School, consultations, „mediumistic" healing journeys, etc.

Martin Brune publishes a monthly contribution on various current and life issues and expresses his opinion from an „energetic" perspective on important questions of our time.

Visit us anytime at:
http://www.shamanic.de/dasbuch.htm

You can contact us with suggestions or proposals at the address: institute@shamanic.de